101 Games That Keep Kids Coming

Get-to-Know-You Games
for Ages 3-12

Jolene L. Roehlkepartain

Abingdon Press
Nashville

GW00985757

101 GAMES THAT KEEP KIDS COMING: GET-TO-KNOW-YOU GAMES FOR AGES 3–12

Copyright © 2008 by Abingdon Press

This book is printed on acid-free paper.

Library of Congress Cataloging-in-Publication Data

Roehlkepartain, Jolene L.,
  101 games that keep kids coming : get-to-know-you games for ages 3-12 / Jolene L. Roehlkepartain.
    p. cm.
  Includes index.
  ISBN 978-0-687-65120-7 (pbk. : alk. paper)
  1. Games in Christian education. 2. Christian education of children. 3. Church work with children. I. Title. II. Title: One hundred and one games that keep kids coming. III. Title: One hundred one games that keep kids coming.

  BV1536.3.R62 2008
  268'.432—dc22

2007018989

All scripture quotations unless noted otherwise are taken from the New Revised Standard Version of the Bible, copyright 1989, Division of Christian Education of the National Council of the Churches of Christ in the United States of America. Used by permission. All rights reserved.

Scripture quotations marked (GNT) are from the Good News Translation in Today's English Version-Second Edition © 1992 by American Bible Society. Used by Permission.

08 09 10 11 12 13 14 15 16 17—10 9 8 7 6 5 4 3 2 1

MANUFACTURED IN THE UNITED STATES OF AMERICA

101 Games
That Keep Kids Coming

To Duane Googins and Gail Miller,
whom all the kids adore because
Duane and Gail are always interested in them

Contents

Introduction

Relationships: The Key to Keeping Kids Coming

W hy do some Christian education programs flourish while others struggle or wither? Leaders of an effective Christian education program know how to encourage children to come—and to keep coming. How? By building relationships among those who come and reaching out to those who rarely or sporadically attend. In *Effective Christian Education: A National Study of Protestant Congregations* (Peter L. Benson and Carolyn H. Eklin [Minneapolis, 1990]), Search Institute researchers concluded that teaching children "how to make friends or be a good friend" and creating a "sense of community" are two key factors in creating effective Christian education. Playing games that encourage children to get to know each other and to build a strong sense of community is an effective and fun way to help children connect. Community-building games get kids excited and keep them coming to more Christian education classes and programs.

The friendship factor is key to attracting children to your Christian education program—and to keeping them coming back. A Gallup/Group Publishing study found that people who are very satisfied with their church:

- Have a best friend at church (87%)
- Report that church leaders seem to care about them (84%)

Building strong relationships between children is important, but so is building community between children and the people who lead programs and classes. "Deep, lasting friendships borne out of faith and nurtured in the church may be the single most effective strategy in reinvigorating the American church," conclude the researchers of the Gallup/Group Publishing study. "Faith grows best in community, and friendships at church

change lives" (Dave Thornton, ed., *Friendship: Creating a Culture of Connectivity in Your Church* [Loveland, Col.: Group Publishing, 2005], 11, 39).

101 Games That Keep Kids Coming includes 101 new games that encourage children to get to know each other—and to build strong friendships. The book includes these major sections:

- Part 1 presents 25 new get-to-know-you games for preschoolers (ages three to five)
- Part 2 includes 25 new get-to-know-you games for children in kindergarten to third grade
- Part 3 gives 25 new get-to-know-you games for children in fourth to sixth grade
- Part 4 includes 26 new get-to-know-you games for mixed ages (children in kindergarten to sixth grade)
- A scripture index
- A topical index

Each game starts out with a topic (the major theme or topic of the game), a scripture passage, the needed familiarity level between children, and a materials list. The familiarity level between children gives you ideas on when to use a specific game. For example, if you have a lot of new children who don't know each other, choose games that have a familiarity level of "none." If you have children who know each other well (and you want them to go deeper with their relationships), choose games that have a familiarity level of "some to a lot."

Many children resist coming to Sunday school and children's ministry events because they simply don't know each other. Many live in different communities and attend different schools. Some attend only sporadically. Playing a lot of getting-to-know-you games and community-building games from this book can boost attendance and form strong friendships between children.

101 Games That Keep Kids Coming will transform your Christian education program into one that's more effective and that gets children talking and coming. So think of playtime as more than fun and games. Think of games as the key to building community—and faith—in children.

"An effective Christian education program has the strongest tie to a person's growth in faith," say Search Institute researchers in *Effective Christian Education*; "nothing matters more than effective Christian education"(2).

Part 1

Great Games for
PRESCHOOLERS

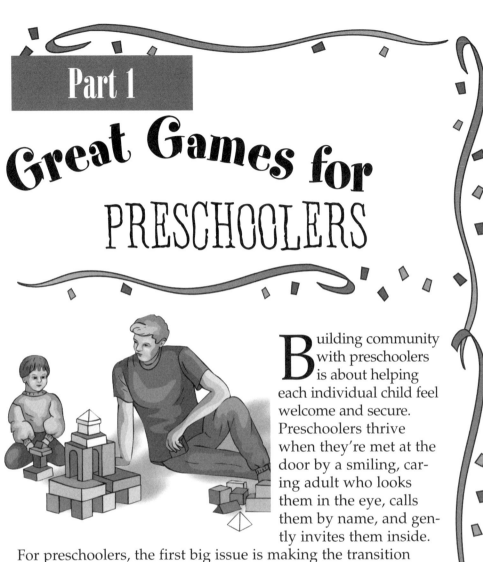

Building community with preschoolers is about helping each individual child feel welcome and secure. Preschoolers thrive when they're met at the door by a smiling, caring adult who looks them in the eye, calls them by name, and gently invites them inside.

For preschoolers, the first big issue is making the transition from the adult who drops them off to the adult who welcomes them to class. Make the transition time smooth by making it easier for them.

Your room can also make transitions easier. Preschoolers are attracted to a room full of interesting toys and bright colors. Instead of expecting preschoolers to sit at a table and wait for the rest of the class to arrive (or get picked up afterward), invite them to explore the toys. Have blocks, four- to six-piece puzzles, dolls, doll clothes, trucks, cars, pegboards, large wooden beads to string, crayons and paper, dress-up clothes, and more.

Once preschoolers are in your room, help children attach to the adults and teenagers who work with your program first. This process of focusing your efforts on individuals may seem slow at first, but it will pay off over time. Parents and grandparents will be thrilled when their preschoolers make the leap of walking into a classroom and going straight for the toys—without the fuss of saying good-bye or not wanting to come. Preschoolers will only do this when they know—and feel comfortable—with the leaders of their class.

Once preschoolers know your leaders and their room, begin building community among the children. Remember that your youngest preschoolers are moving from the developmental stage of parallel play (where they play individually side by side) to simple cooperative play (where they play with each other for short amounts of time interspersed with individual play). Begin by teaching children each other's names through the games in this section.

Your older preschoolers will begin connecting more with each other, and you may even see some close friendships develop. Encourage this whenever you can. Sometimes best friends are the same sex, but sometimes they're not. Let children lead the way in finding their friends, but create many opportunities for them to mingle with different children and see what develops.

With preschoolers, schedule short play times where children can choose what to play and who they want to play with. Although young children thrive on structure, they also thrive when they're given structured times to explore, to play, and to interact with other children.

However you choose to build community, have fun with your preschoolers. Help them feel comfortable, but also get down on the floor to play and laugh with them. Soon you'll have kids crawling in and out of your lap and forming a close-knit community around you. That's what you want: happy preschoolers who want to keep coming back, week after week.

When You Hear the Name

Topic: Names
Scripture: Mark 14:66-72
Familiarity Between Children: None to a lot
Materials: None

1

Game: Have the children sit on the floor. Say, "I'm going to read you a story from the Bible. Every time you hear the word *rooster*, jump up and say, 'cock-a-doodle-doo.' Then sit down and listen for the word again." Read aloud Mark 14:66-72. Pause slightly every time you read the word *rooster*.

After you read the passage, say that you're going to name children. When a child hears his or her name, that child should jump up and shout out his or her first name followed by shouting, "That's me!" Then the child should sit down.

Let the children try this. Explain that periodically you'll say the word *rooster*, and everyone should jump up and say, "cock-a-doodle-doo."

Play the game. After awhile, end the game by naming all the children's names quickly and saying, "Now let's be like roosters and strut back to our lesson."

Silly Time

Topic: Time, being silly
Scripture: Ecclesiastes 3
Familiarity Between Children: None to a little
Materials: None

Game: Say, "Ecclesiastes 3 says there is a time for everything. There is a time to be happy and sad, and there is a time to be silly and goofy. We're going to be silly while we get to know each other."

Have the children stand in a circle.

Say, "We're going to take turns doing or saying something silly. When I call on you, be silly and then we'll do the same silly action that you do."

Demonstrate before you play. Explain that each time, everyone will say this phrase:

"Louie, Louie, (_Name of Child twice_), Silly Dilly
Can you show us something silly?"

Then have Louie (or the child named) do something silly, such as make monkey sounds, wiggle his or her body in a funny way, snort like a pig, make a silly face, or do something else that's completely goofy. After the child does something silly, have everyone do the exact same silly action or noise.

End the turn by having everyone say, "Louie, Louie, (_Name of Child_), you're so silly."

Have children take turns at being silly. Encourage them to learn each other's names.

End the game by saying your name. Do a silly action, such as making a burping sound or saying "look's like we're a crazy group" but starting each word with a _w_ sound: "wook's wike we're wa wrazy wroup."

Ring, Ring

Topic: Communication
Scripture: Matthew 6:6-13
Familiarity Between Children: None to a lot
Materials: A toy phone

Game: Have the children stand in a circle. Say, "We're going to play a game with a toy phone. What do you do when the phone rings?" Let them answer. Then say, "For this game when the phone rings, I want you to say, 'Hello, this is (*Your Name*).' Pay close attention because later on you'll need to say the other children's names."

Hold the phone. Make a ringing sound. Give the phone to one child who then answers it. After the child does it, take the phone back and repeat with another child. Continue until all the children have answered the phone at least once.

Once each child has had a turn, change the game. Say, "Now we're going to play the game in another way. I'm going to give someone the phone. Make a ringing sound and name a child in the circle. That child will jump up to answer it. After that child answers, stop making the ringing sound. Then the child who answered will take the phone, make it ring, and say another child's name. That child will jump up and answer, and so on."

Play the game. Do this until each child has had at least one turn.

End the game by asking, "How do we talk to God?" Get children's ideas. Ask if they can call God on the telephone. Then talk about prayer. End with the prayer, "Thank you, God, for being with us and helping us get to know each other."

3

Leaping Leaders

Topic: Leadership
Scripture: Numbers 2
Familiarity Between Children: None to a lot
Materials: None

Game: Ask the children to stand in a circle. Say, "The Bible is full of people who were leaders. We're going to take turns being the leader. When I point to you, say your name and name one action that we can do. For example, you could say hop, leap, jump, run, wiggle, and so on."

Start the game. Sometimes a child may have the children run and break up the circle. If that happens, have the circle form again once the children finish running. Give each child one turn.

When everyone has had one turn, ask, "Who remembers someone's name and action?" If a child can identify another child's name and motion correctly, have the group do that motion again. End the activity by saying, "Each one of us was a leaping leader. Let's all leap back to our lesson."

Spin

Topic: Names
Scripture: Luke 11:9-13
Familiarity Between Children: None to a lot
Materials: None

Game: Have the children stand in a circle. Ask for a volunteer to stand in the middle. Say, "The Bible says that when you ask, you will receive. When you seek, you will find. When you knock, the door will be opened to you. We're going to play a game where we'll learn each other's names better."

Explain that the child in the middle will say either "shout" or "whisper" before spinning around and pointing at someone. All the children will then either shout or whisper the name of the child whom the volunteer is pointing to.

Play the game. Have the volunteer do this three times and then ask for another volunteer. Children will gradually learn each other's names as you play.
End the game by saying, "Let's all shout the word *group* and then give each other a big group hug."

Sing Together

Topic: Names, friendship
Scripture: Proverbs 22:1
Familiarity Between Children: None to a lot
Materials: None

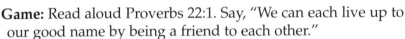

Game: Read aloud Proverbs 22:1. Say, "We can each live up to our good name by being a friend to each other."

Have the children sing together these words to the tune of "Skip to My Lou" as they hold hands in a circle and skip to the right.

> Skip, skip, skip with my friends
> Skip, skip, skip with my friends
> Skip, skip, skip with my friends
> We are all such good friends.

When the children have finished singing the song once, tell them that you'll sing the song again. This time when they finish the song, you'll point to one child and that child will quickly shout out his or her first name. The child on the right will do the same, and you'll keep going around the circle until every child has shouted out his or her first name.

Sing the song again and ask for a volunteer to try to name as many children as possible.

End the game by saying, "We are all such good friends, and when we skip and play together, we have more fun."

6

Who Do We Appreciate?

Topic: Compliments
Scripture: 2 Corinthians 6:6
Familiarity Between Children: None to a lot
Materials: None

7

Game: Have the children form a circle and stand. Read aloud 2 Corinthians 6:6. Teach them this chant:

> Two, four, six, eight
> Who do we appreciate?
> One, three, five, nine
> Who right here is mighty fine?

Once the children know the chant, say that there is a second part to the chant. After the chant, you'll point to one child, and all the children will shout that child's name three times. For example, the chant could go like this:

> Two, four, six, eight
> Who do we appreciate?
> One, three, five, nine
> Who right here is mighty fine?
> Lisa! Lisa! Lisa!

Do the chant a number of times with different children's names. Once the children know the chant really well, challenge them further by choosing three different children for the ending chant, so they would say something like: Harry! Gina! Jorge!

Note that one child may notice that the chant leaves out the number seven. If someone notices, see if the group can figure out why the chant goes from one, three, five, nine and isn't three, five, seven, nine. (This has to do with the number of syllables in each word and the rhyme.)

End the activity by doing the chant one last time, except for shouting out God! God! God! at the end.

What I Like about You

Topic: Compliments
Scripture: Genesis 12:11
Familiarity Between Children: Some to a lot
Materials: None

Game: Have the children sit in a circle. Say, "In the book of Genesis, Abram told his wife Sarai that she was beautiful. We're going to go around the circle and say something nice about someone. You can say something simple, such as, 'I like your blue dress' or something that you know about the person, such as 'I like that you hum a lot.' When it's your turn, point to the child you want to say something nice about, say his or her name if you know it, and then say something nice."

Play the game. If a child says something inappropriate, be ready to jump in with a compliment. You may also want to consider having children talk faster and move around the circle faster to make the game livelier.

End the game by saying, "I am very glad that you notice and say nice things to each other. I always like spending time with people who are nice to me, don't you?"

Thank You!

What We Do Together

Topic: Working together, disciples
Scripture: Acts 14:21-23
Familiarity Between Children: None to a lot
Materials: None

9

Game: Read aloud Acts 14:21-23. Explain that when the disciples worked together, they got more done.

Have the children form two groups. Have them line up on one side of the room behind a starting line.

Designate a finish line at the other side of the room. Clear the area between.

Say, "When I tell you to go, the first person in line will shout out his or her first name and then jump as far as he or she can. Then the rest of the group will join that child, and the second person in line will shout out his or her first name and then jump as far as he or she can. Each time a child finishes a jump, the rest of the group joins that child, and then the next person in line makes the next jump. Keep jumping until you get to the finish line."

If the children enjoy the game, form new teams and have them play the game again.

End the activity by saying, "When we work together like the disciples did, we make a lot of progress. All of you were great jumpers today."

Who Are You?

Topic: Thanksgiving
Scripture: 1 Chronicles 16:34
Familiarity Between Children: None to a little
Materials: A beanbag or small ball for every six kids

Game: Have the children stand in a circle. If you have more than eight children present, create groups of six children.

Say, "The Bible says it is good to give thanks. We're going to play a thanksgiving game. First we're going to get to know each other." Give a beanbag or ball to one child in each circle. Have the children toss the beanbag or ball to another child in the circle while saying his or her own first name. After they do this awhile, change the game.

Say, "Now I want you to name something you're thankful for. When you get the beanbag (or ball) say your name again and one thing you're thankful for. Then toss the beanbag (or ball) to someone else."

After awhile, end the activity by saying, "It is good to give thanks to God. Let's all say, Amen. Amen!"

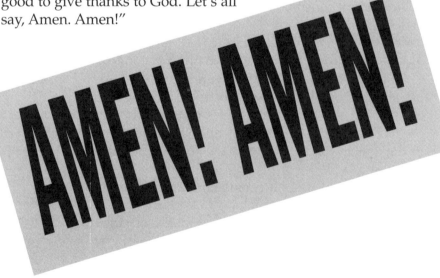

Who Do You Know?

Topic: Friendship
Scripture: John 15:15-17
Familiarity Between Children: None to a lot
Materials: None

Game: Read aloud John 15:15-17. Say that everyone is a friend and that we should love one another.

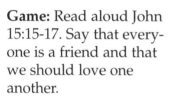

Have the children sit in a circle. Teach them this song to the tune of "Row, Row, Row Your Boat":

> You, You, You, I know
> We know everyone.
> Thank you, Thank you, Thank you, God
> For our good, good friends.

Once the children know the song, explain that each time the group sings the song, you're going to point to a child in the circle. That child then jumps up and stands while everyone shouts that child's first name aloud. Have the child remain standing while you sing the song again. Sing the song over and over until every child is standing.

End the activity by having all the children sit. Ask, "Who are our good friends?" then point to a child in the circle who jumps up while everyone shouts that child's name. Slowly move around the circle so that children are jumping up one after another.

So Many Ways to Move

Topic: Trust
Scripture: Exodus 14:15-18
Familiarity Between Children: None to a lot
Materials: None

12

Game: Summarize Exodus 14:15-18 by saying, "At one time, the bad guys were after the good guys in the Bible. The good guys were scared, and God said that if they trusted God and kept moving, God would keep them safe."

Explain that you're going to play a moving game. Have the children spread throughout the room. Tell them that you're going to name a type of person and they should move like that person would. Name people such as these (one at a time):

- A baby
- An old person with a cane
- (Name one of the children in your group who will pick a motion and everyone else will follow it.)
- An Olympic runner
- (Name another child in your group who will pick a motion and everyone else will follow it.)
- A swimmer
- (Name another child in your group who will pick a motion and everyone else will follow it.)
- A person without any legs

End the activity by saying, "Whether we walk, crawl, limp, or run, God is always with us. We can always trust God."

Jingle Good Time

Topic: Good example
Scripture: Philippians 3:17
Familiarity Between Children: None to some
Materials: Jingle bells for each child

Game: Read aloud Philippians 3:17. Talk about how important it is to set a good example. Besides being nice to each other, we can also set a good example by playing together and helping children feel included.

Give each child some jingle bells. Teach them these slightly different words to the tune of "Jingle Bells":

> Jingle Bells. Jingle Bells.
> Jingle all the way.
> Oh, what fun it is to have
> (<u>*Name of Child*</u>) join us today.

Once the children know the new words, have them sit on the floor throughout the room. Say you'll start singing this song alone while ringing your jingle bells. When children hear their names called, they can jump up and join you with the singing and ringing.

Move around the room as you sing the song. If you have only a few children present, name only one child at a time. If you have a lot of children, name two or three at a time.

13

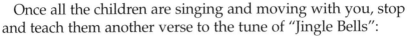

Once all the children are singing and moving with you, stop and teach them another verse to the tune of "Jingle Bells":

> Jingle Bells. Jingle Bells.
> Jingle all the way.
> Oh, what fun it is to have
> (*Name of Child*) fall off the sleigh.

Explain that everyone will sing and move with you and when you name a child to fall off the sleigh, he or she should dramatically drop from the group and sit quietly on the floor. Play the game until all the children have returned to the floor.

End the activity by saying, "We set good examples when we include everyone when we play and when we sing together." Let the children ring their jingle bells loudly one last time before you collect the bells.

Who Is Hiding?

Topic: Hiding
Scripture: Joshua 10:16-17
Familiarity Between Children: None to some
Materials: None

Game: Say, "In the Bible, there were a group of people who hid in caves. Then Joshua found them. It was like a game of hide and seek."

Have the children stand in a circle. Go around the circle and have each child say his or her name aloud. Then say, "Closely look at what each person is wearing. We're going to play a game of hide and seek, and you'll need to figure out who is hiding without finding that person."

Teach children this chant:

> Who is hiding? Who is hiding?
> Who can it be?
> Who is hiding? Who is hiding?
> It's (_Name of Child_)! See!

Explain that whoever knows who is missing can run to where the hiding child is and point him or her out.

Have the children line up facing one wall. Have them close their eyes. Then quietly choose one child and have that child hide somewhere in the room. Once the child is hidden, have the other children uncover their eyes and turn around. Begin the chant. Pause before the last line to see if anyone has any guesses. If no one knows, ask the hiding child to jump out and say, "It's (_Name of Child_), see!"

Play again with a different hiding child. Play a number of times.

End the activity by saying, "Sometimes we hide when we're scared. Sometimes we hide when we're upset. Sometimes we hide to play, but God always knows where we are. We can never hide from God."

Thankful for Everyone

Topic: Thanksgiving
Scripture: 1 Thessalonians 5:16-18
Familiarity Between Children: None to a lot
Materials: None

15

Game: Have the children stand in a circle. Help them memorize a paraphrase of 1 Thessalonians 5:16-18 and actions that go with it. Teach them:

Be joyful. (*Smile.*)
Pray always.
(*Fold hands and bow your heads.*)

Thank God for everything. (*Hold hands and go around the circle and name one thing you're thankful for.*)

After the children have done this, end the activity by having them slightly change the last part of the paraphrase to this:

Be joyful. (*Smile.*)
Pray always. (*Fold hands and bow your heads.*)
Thank God for everyone. (*Hold hands and go around the circle, and everyone says his or her first name aloud.*)

So Many Emotions

Topic: Emotions, feelings
Scripture: Ecclesiastes 3:1-15
Familiarity Between Children: None to a lot
Materials: None

Game: Talk about Ecclesiastes 3:1-15 and how there is a time for every emotion: anger, sadness, happiness, disgust, surprise, fear, excitement, and more. Say you're going to play a feelings game. Have the children sit in a circle.

Teach children this chant:

> Sometimes we're happy.
> Sometimes we're sad.
> What kind of face does (_Name of Child_) make
> when he (or she) is (*name an emotion: sad, angry,*
> *happy, disgusted, surprised, excited, scared, or sick*).

Once children know the chant, choose a child and an emotion each time during that part of the chant. Once children have finished, you can change the game and have children make the sounds of different emotions.

End the activity by saying, "Whether we're happy or sad, angry or excited, God is always with us."

16

Squished Together

Topic: Welcome others
Scripture: Hebrews 13:1-3
Familiarity Between Children: None to a lot
Materials: A chair for each child and music that you can quickly turn on and off

Game: Set up a game of musical chairs. Make a circle with the chairs facing out. Have one fewer chairs than you have children.

Say, "Hebrews 13:1-3 says that it's good to welcome everyone. We're going to play a game of musical chairs. When the music stops, find a chair. If all the chairs are taken, find a child who is sitting and sit in that child's lap."

Have the children make a circle around the chairs. Have them march around the chairs while the music plays. Then suddenly stop the music. Watch what happens. Then remove another chair and make the circle tighter. Say, "We'll play again. This time two different children will be sitting on the laps of two children. Ready?"

Play again. Continue removing one chair each time you play again so that more and more children have to sit on each other's laps. Play until you're down to one chair (or a couple of chairs if you have a large group) so that most children are sitting on each other's laps.

End the activity by saying, "Let's find out who is squished!" Have the child at the top stand and say his or her name aloud. Then have the next sitting child do the same, and so on. Clap after the last child stands up and says his or her name.

Great Names

Topic: Names
Scripture: Proverbs 3:1-4
Familiarity Between Children: None to a lot
Materials: None

Game: Have children sit in a circle. Read aloud Proverbs 3:1-4. Talk about making a good name for yourself by getting to know others and paying attention to them.

18

Say, "We're going to play a name game. When I call out your name, stand for three seconds, and then sit down. While the person stands, let's repeat the child's name in the same manner that I called out the name. Listen closely."

Before you begin, teach the kids to tap their legs twice and clap, tap their legs twice and clap, and continue to keep this steady beat.

Name children (one at a time), in one of these different ways:
- Shouting
- Whispering
- Speaking high like a squeaky mouse
- Speaking low and slow like a talking elephant
- Saying a name quickly
- Saying a name slowly
- Saying a name while changing the pitch of your voice with each syllable, such as saying Stephanie with "Steph" being high "an" being low and "ie" being high again
- Saying one name and then another name right after it
- Saying three names in a row

End the activity by saying, "We all have great names. It's fun to make different sounds with our names and get to know each other a bit more."

Picture Pass

Topic: Jesus
Scripture: Matthew 28:20
Familiarity Between Children: None to a lot
Materials: A picture of Jesus

19

Game: Read aloud Matthew 28:20. Talk about how Jesus is with you no matter where you go.

Have the children sit in a circle. Have them practice passing the picture around the circle. Then play the game. Say, "We're going to take turns holding the picture. Whenever someone holds the picture, we'll say a chant that names the child twice before the child finishes the chant by naming one place where Jesus is with that person. For example, Jesus can be with you at home, at the grocery store, in the car, on the bus, anywhere you can think of!"

Practice this saying with one child holding the picture of Jesus:

Jesus is with (*everyone names the child holding the picture*) whenever (*everyone names the child holding the picture*) is at (*a place that the child holding the picture names*).

Here's an example: Jesus is with <u>Danny</u> whenever <u>Danny plays outside</u>.

Once the children know the chant, have them take turns passing the picture of Jesus around the circle. Instead of having the picture stop with each child, let the children pass the picture until you say "stop." Then do the chant together and have the child holding the picture name a place where Jesus is with him or her. Do this until each child has had a turn.

End the activity by saying, "No matter where we go, Jesus is always with us."

Good News

Topic: Self-esteem, communication
Scripture: Psalm 139
Familiarity Between Children: None to a lot
Materials: A beanbag

Game: Summarize Psalm 139 by saying something like, "God knows everything about you. God even knew you when you were inside your mom. Now let's tell some good news about ourselves to each other."

Have the children sit in a circle. Give one child a beanbag. Have the children pass the beanbag around the circle while singing "When You're Happy and You Know It." Whoever is holding the beanbag at the end of the verse, stops the song, says his or her first name aloud, and then says something great that has happened (or is about to happen) to him or her. For example, maybe a grandmother is coming for a visit, or someone's dad bought ice cream, or someone got a new toy, or someone is going on a trip, and so on. When the child finishes, have everyone say together, "That's great, (_Name of Child_)!"

God knows you.
Psalm 139

Then start singing the song again and passing the beanbag around the circle. If a child gets the beanbag again, he or she can give the beanbag to another child who has not had a turn. Play the game until everyone has had a turn.

End the activity by saying, "We're all happy, and we know it! God gives us many good things, and it's good to share our good news with others."

Listen Closely

Topic: Listening
Scripture: James 1:22-25
Familiarity Between Children: None to a lot
Materials: Music that you can easily turn on and off

Game: Read aloud James 1:22-25. Talk about how important it is to listen closely.

Have the children spread throughout the room. Say, "We're going to play a listening game. When you hear music playing, jog around the room. As soon as you hear the music stop, freeze, and shout out your first name. The last person who shouts out his or her first name will step out of the game and wait along the side. Then we'll play again to see who's the slowest to listen, and we'll keep playing until we have the best listener left."

Play the game. When one child is left, congratulate him or her.

End the activity by saying, "When we listen closely, we know what to do next. Let's keep our listening ears working as we move to the next part of our lesson."

Never Alone

Topic: Fear, friendship
Scripture: 1 Samuel 17
Familiarity Between Children: None to a lot
Materials: None

Game: Summarize the story of David and Goliath found in 1 Samuel 17. Talk about how afraid David was of Goliath and how it's easy to get scared.

Have children stand in a circle. Choose one child to stand in the middle. Have that child say, "I (_Name of Child_) am never alone." Then have that child choose another child to stand in the middle with him or her. Have the two children standing in the middle say together, "We (_Name of First Child and then Name of Second Child_) are never alone."

Ask the newest member of the middle choose another child. Again, have the three children say, "We (_Name of First Child, then Name of Second Child, then Name of Third Child_) are never alone."

Continue playing the game until everyone is in the middle of the circle.

End the game by saying, "No matter how scared we get, God is always with us. We also have many friends who will be with us when we are afraid."

Helping Others

Topic: Helping, Good Samaritan
Scripture: Luke 10:30-37
Familiarity Between Children: None to a lot
Materials: Lots of Band-Aid® or similar bandages for each child

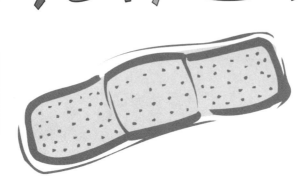

Game: Before you play the game, remove the outer wrapper from each bandage. Give each child at least one bandage for every child present. For example, if you have eight children present, give each child eight bandages.

Say, "Each one of you is God's helper. In the Bible, there is a story about the good Samaritan. He stopped to help someone who was hurt along the road. We're going to play a game about being good helpers."

Have the children spread throughout the room and walk around. Say, "When I yell out a name, go to that child and place one of your bandages on him or her. Stick them only on skin or clothes, not in anyone's hair."

Have the children walk around. Periodically name a child. Once children have finished putting the bandages on that child, have them all walk around again. Continue calling out names until every child has been called, and every child is covered with bandages.

End the game by saying, "Whenever someone is hurt, we can help. You were all great helpers today."

Animal Crack-ups

Topic: Animals
Scripture: Genesis 1:20-25
Familiarity Between Children: None to a lot
Materials: Lots of animal crackers

24

Game: Talk about God creating all the animals in the world, according to Genesis 1:20-25. Have the children sit in a circle. Give each child an animal cracker, and encourage the children not to show which animal they received. Say, "We're going to take turns going around the circle. When it's your turn, say your first name and then make the sound of your animal cracker. Then the rest of us will guess the animal. Let us know when we make the right guess."

Start with one child and play the game. Keep track of the different animals.

After every child has had a turn, say, "If you have a lion, stand." Have those children each say their first name and sit together. (You'll have to have children move around some.) Then name another animal and do the same thing. Continue doing this until all the animal cracker animals have been named and kids are sitting together according to animal type.

End the game by letting children eat their animal crackers. Distribute more animal crackers to those who are hungry.

Lovable Kids

Topic: God's children
Scripture: Romans 8:16-17
Familiarity Between Children: None to a lot
Materials: A sheet of inexpensive stickers for each child in the shape of hearts or smiling faces

25

Game: Read aloud Romans 8:16-17. Talk about how each one of us is God's child.

Give each child a sheet of stickers. Have the children spread throughout the room. Say, "When I tell you to go, I want you to move around the room and place a sticker on each person. As you do this say, 'I like you.' If you know the child's name, say that child's name. Once you have placed a sticker on each person, keep moving around the room and place stickers on people until all your stickers are gone. You can place stickers on everyone but yourself."

Play the game. Children soon will be giggling about becoming covered with stickers.

End the activity by saying, "Each one of you is special. Each one of you is lovable. Look at you! You're covered with stickers that show how much everyone cares about you."

Part 2

Great Games for
YOUNG CHILDREN

C hildren in the younger elementary-school grades (from
kindergarten to third grade) are like sponges. They're
soaking up everything. They're learning the alphabet.
They're learning to read. They're learning to add and subtract.
They're learning more and more words.

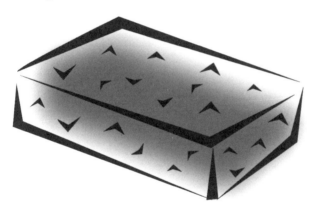

They're also learning more about being with other children. In
fact, so many social skills are learned and mastered between
kindergarten and third grade that researchers say that children's
adeptness in getting along with others is a key factor in their
development. Researchers in the *Journal of Clinical and Consulting
Psychology* have found that how popular a child is in third grade
is a better predictor of how mentally healthy the child will be at
age eighteen than any other factor. Helping children make and
keep friends, teaching them to resolve conflicts in peaceful ways,
and showing them how to manage their emotions in positive

ways are all key ways to help children grow up well and get along with others.

This isn't always easy, however, when some children are shy and withdrawn, others have problems with being impulsive, and others have emotional and physical disabilities. Sometimes you may need extra volunteers to assist you, particularly if you have one or two children who try to dominate or pull the group off track.

No matter what type of group dynamics you have, get to know each child individually. Help children get to know each other so that they make friends. Your other goals of teaching children about the Bible and about Christian living will happen more easily when children feel at home in your group, are known by others in your group, and look forward to coming because they have friends in your group.

Double Trouble

Topic: Jesus, nicknames
Scripture: Isaiah 9:6
Familiarity Between Children: Some to a lot
Materials: A ball that is soft (or a beanbag)

26

Game: Read aloud Isaiah 9:6. As a group, have the children identify nicknames for Jesus from the scripture.

Then say, "A lot of people have nicknames. We're going to play a game about our names and nicknames. If you don't have a nickname, tell us your middle name. If you don't have a nickname or a middle name, then use your last name as the second name."

Give one child the ball (or beanbag). Have the child say his or her first name and nickname (or middle name or last name) before giving the ball to the person on his or her right. Continue around the circle until everyone has had a turn. Encourage the children to pay close attention to the other children's names and nicknames.

Ask for a volunteer. Give the child the ball. Have the child walk around the circle, look into each child's eyes (one at a time), and say the child's first name and nickname. See how many children the child can correctly identify before making a mistake. When the child makes a mistake, the misnamed child stands up (while the other child takes his or her place). Then that child goes around the circle as far as he or she can.

Cheer any child who can name every person correctly. Play the game a number of times so that the children can practice.

End the game by saying, "It's tricky to learn two names for each person. You did a great job. Let's hear it for knowing each other's names and nicknames." As a group, clap and cheer.

Wonderful You

Topic: Self-esteem
Scripture: 1 Timothy 4:4
Familiarity Between Children: None to a little
Materials: None

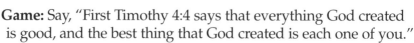

27

Game: Say, "First Timothy 4:4 says that everything God created is good, and the best thing that God created is each one of you."

Have the children spread throughout the room and sit down. Explain that you're going to name different amazing things, and if that thing describes you, do the action.

Start with one example. Say, "Everyone who loves to play, stand up." See who stands up.

Say the following statements and actions. If only a few children do the action, have those children say their names aloud, so that the children can learn each other's names. After each statement and action, have the children sit down.

- If you have a dog, jump up and bark.
- If you have a brother, stand up and lift your hands above your head.
- If your favorite color is blue, jump up and down.
- If you like to play outside, hop on one foot.
- If you have a cat, stand up and meow.
- If you have a sister, stand up and hold hands with someone who is standing.
- If your favorite color is red, run around the room.
- If you have a pet that is not a cat or dog, stand up and smile. (Then ask each child standing what kind of pet he or she has.)
- If you like books, stand up and wiggle your body.
- If you love God, jump up and shout, "Amen!"

End the game by saying, "God made each one of us in a wonderful way. Let's jump up and shout hooray!"

Links of Love

Topic: Love
Scripture: Amos 5:14-15
Familiarity Between Children: None to a lot
Materials: Colored construction paper, washable markers, and
filled staplers

Game: Before you do this game, cut colored construction paper
into two-inch wide strips. (If you have a paper cutter, this can
go quickly.)

Have the children sit at tables where they can reach colored
construction paper strips and markers. Say, "The Bible says it is
good to love things that make us better people." Have each
child write his or her name on one of the colored strips. Then
say, "We're each going to make a necklace showing what we
love. On a strip of paper, write or draw one thing you love. For
example, you might draw a dog on one strip and then draw a
book on another strip if you like to read. Make about ten strips of
ten different things you love."

When the children finish, help them assemble their paper
chains with the ten things they love and their name. Create a
necklace for each one to wear. Ask the chil-
dren to take turns telling the group
what is on their necklaces.

End the activity by saying,
"Think about all the things
you love as you wear
your links of
love."

Which Is You?

Topic: Self-esteem
Scripture: Philemon 4-7
Familiarity Between Children: None to a lot
Materials: Two large pieces of colored construction paper
(choose two colors that are different such as red and
yellow or blue and orange or green and yellow),
blue painter's tape

29

Game: Hang up one piece of colored construction paper on
one end of the room and the other on the other end of the
room. Hang the pieces of paper so they're about eye level with
the children.

Say, "In the Bible, Paul wrote a letter to his good friend Philemon. In the letter, Paul tells what he loves about Philemon. We're going to learn more about each other to find out what's so interesting about each other."

Have the children stand in the middle of the room between the places where the paper is hung. Point out the locations of the two pieces of colored paper on the wall. Explain that you're going to give the children two choices. They need to run to the color that best fits their answer. Explain that they may either stay in the same place or run to the other color when another statement is read.

Choose topics such as these and say the colors that you hung up. These examples include the colors red and yellow:

- If you're a boy, run to the red. If you're a girl, run to the yellow.
- If you like morning better than nighttime, run to the red. If you like nighttime better than morning, run to the yellow.
- If you like to play inside more than you like to play outside, run to the red. If you like play outside more than you like to play inside, run to the yellow.
- If you like breakfast better than dinner, run to the red. If you like dinner better than breakfast, run to the yellow.
- If you like to play alone rather than with someone, run to the red. If you like play with someone rather than play alone, run to the yellow.

Periodically pause and have the children shout out their names at each color.

End the activity by saying, "I'm glad you know yourselves so well. We all have things we like better than others. Sometimes we meet friends when we're doing activities we like, which makes the activity even more fun."

One to Six

Topic: Self-esteem
Scripture: Psalm 63:2-5
Familiarity Between Children: None to a lot
Materials: A die for about every six children

Game: Create groups of about six children. If you have ten children present or fewer, use one die and play together.

Say, "We're going to play a game to get to know each other better. We're going to take turns rolling the die. Whatever number you get, tell us that many things about you. For example, if I got the number three, I would tell you that I like pizza, playing with my cat, and singing (*give three examples about yourself*)." If children do not know each other's names, have them first say their name before they say things about themselves.

Play the game. Do this until each child has had a turn. If children have difficulty naming things, focus on a specific topic, such as one of these:

- Which activities do you enjoy most?
- What are you favorite toys?
- What are your favorite foods?
- What do you like to do on the weekend?
- Who are your favorite people?

End the activity by saying, "We heard a lot of great things about each other. Now let's go around the circle and name one thing that we love about God." Once everyone has done this, say, "Amen."

Colorful Touch

Topic: Colors
Scripture: Genesis 9:1-17
Familiarity Between Children: None to a lot
Materials: None

Game: Have the children form two groups. Have each group stand in a line about six feet from the other group.

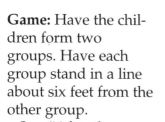

Say, "After the flood, God told Noah that a rainbow of color would show that God would never again flood the earth. A rainbow is beautiful. It has every color in it. We're going to play a game about colors."

Give one group one name and the other group another name. For example, you might call the group on your right, group one, and the group on your left, group two.

Say, "I'm going to name a color and a group number. If you're part of that group, walk over to a child in the other group who is wearing that color. Touch the color. If you know the child's name, say it aloud. If you don't, ask for the child's name."

Play the game. Alternate between the groups, and call out these colors:

- Red
- Yellow
- Green
- Black
- Brown
- Blue
- Orange
- Purple
- White
- Pink

End the game by saying, "God made so many wonderful colors. Not only do you know your colors well, but you're also getting to know the names of the children in this group."

Crazy Chairs

Topic: Friendship
Scripture: John 13:11-17
Familiarity Between Children: None to a lot
Materials: A chair for each child

Game: Form a circle with the chairs. Stand in the middle of the circle. Say, "Jesus had twelve disciples, and he was very good friends with them. We're going to play a game about friends. I'm going to start the game by saying the phrase, 'I like everybody here, but I really like people who . . . and then I'll name something specific, such as, are wearing pants.' If you fit that description, you need to jump up and run for another chair. The trick, however, is that I will also be trying to sit in a chair. The last person left gets to be in the middle and name the next thing."

Play the game. Encourage the children to name things, such as these:

- A birthday during a certain month (such as July)
- Anyone who plays soccer
- Anyone who has a mom
- Anyone who is wearing tennis shoes
- Anyone who is seven years old
- Anyone who goes to school
- Anyone who wears glasses

End the game by saying, "It's fun to play together. We have a lot in common. There were a lot of times when most of us were scrambling for a chair."

Mad, Sad, Glad

Topic: Emotions, feelings
Scripture: Psalm 18:6-27
Familiarity Between Children: Some to a lot
Materials: Six index cards, a marker

33

Game: Before you play this game, write on the six index cards. On two cards draw a happy face with the word *glad*. On two other cards draw a sad face with the word *sad*. On the last two cards draw an angry face with the word *mad*. Mix up the cards and have them in a pile, face down.

Have the children form a circle. Have them go around the circle and say their first name aloud. Say, "In the Bible, God sometimes gets mad, sad, and glad. God has feelings, and we all have feelings. We're going to talk about

the feelings we have. We're going to take turns. The first person will draw a card from this stack (the index cards). Talk about what makes you feel this way. When you're finished, add your card to the bottom and pass the stack to the child on your right."

Do the activity until each child has had a turn. End the activity by saying, "Some things make us mad. Let's make an angry face (*Pause*). Some things make us sad. Let's make a sad face (*Pause*). Other things make us happy. Let's make a happy face (*Pause*). God loves us no matter how we feel."

Nametag Mix-up

Topic: Names
Scripture: Philippians 2:9
Familiarity Between Children: None to a little
Materials: A nametag for each child and a marker

34

Game: Once you know who is present, write the name of each child on a separate nametag. Have the children sit in a circle, and give each child a nametag that is not his or her own.

Say, "Philippians 2:9 says that the name of Jesus is greater than any other name. Our names are important. When I tell you to go, I want you to get up and find the child who has your nametag. Find out the name of the child who has your nametag. Then ask for your nametag and put it on your chest.

Keep looking around the room to find the child whose nametag you are holding."

Do this until every child has his or her correct nametag.

End the activity by having the children sit in a circle with their nametags on. Say, "Let's go around the circle. When it's your turn, stand up and say your name and one thing that you love to do." When everyone has done this say, "I'm so glad each one of you is here."

Fast Forward to the Future

Topic: Future
Scripture: Ecclesiastes 8:6-7
Familiarity Between Children: None to a lot
Materials: None

Game: Have the children sit in a circle. Read aloud Ecclesiastes 8:6-7. Explain how no one knows what will happen in the future, but we can play a game where we guess what the future might be like.

Have the children take turns talking about one of these future questions:

- Do you think you'll get married? Why or why not?
- Do you think you'll have children? If so, how many?
- What job do you want to have? Why?
- Where will you live? Why?
- What will you do to help people? Why?
- How often will you go to church? Why?
- How do you want to make the world a better place? Why?

End the activity by saying, "No one knows what the future holds, but it's fun to think about. No matter what happens to us, God is with us. God was with us yesterday. God is with us today, and God will be with us for every one of our tomorrows."

Four Corners

Topic: Fellowship, community
Scripture: 1 Corinthians 1:10-17
Familiarity Between Children: None to a lot
Materials: Four pieces of construction paper: one in red, one in
yellow, one in blue, and one in green; and blue
painter's tape

Game: Hang one piece of colored construction paper in each of the four corners of your room. Have the children gather in the middle of the room.

Say, "The Bible says that even though we are different, it's good to stick together. Let's learn more about each other with this game."

Tell the children to listen closely. Explain that they will run to one corner of the room, depending on their answer to what you say. You may want to read the list twice so the children will know where they are going before they run. Use these groupings, one at a time:

• If you have a winter birthday during the months of December, January, or February, run to the red corner. If you have a spring birthday during the months of March, April, or May, run to the yellow corner. If you have a summer birthday during the months of June, July, or August, run to the blue corner. If you have an autumn birthday during the months of September, October, or November, run to the green corner. (Once children get to their corners, have them take turns saying their first names and giving the month and date of their birthdays.)

- If you are the oldest child in your family, run to the red corner. If you're the youngest child in your family, run to the yellow corner. If you're one of the middle children in your family, run to the blue corner. If you're the only child in your family, run to the green corner. (Once children get to their corners, have them take turns saying their first names and telling a little bit about their families.)

- If you like the winter season best, run to the red corner. If you like the spring season best, run to the yellow corner. If you like the summer season best, run to the blue corner. If you like the autumn season best, run to the green corner. (Once children get to their corners, have them take turns saying their first names and saying why they like that season best.)

End the activity by saying, "Each one of you has a different birthday. Each one of you has a different family. Each one of you

likes a different season. Yet, even though we have these differences, it's good to stick together and play together."

What's in Common?

Topic: Friendship
Scripture: Proverbs 18:24
Familiarity Between Children: None to a lot
Materials: None

37

Game: Read aloud Proverbs 18:24. Ask the children what a good friend is like.

Have each child find a partner. Say, "I want you to talk and try to find one thing that you have in common. Maybe you both like to read books. Maybe you both have broken an arm. Keep talking until you find something in common."

Give the children time to do this. After awhile, have the children find another partner and do the same thing.

Do this a number of times.

End the activity by asking the children what they learned about each other.

Then have the children form a circle and hold hands. Bow your heads and pray. Say, "Thank you, God, for giving us good friends and for giving us things in common. Amen."

Mystery Puzzles

Topic: Mysteries, secrets
Scripture: Ephesians 3:1-6
Familiarity Between Children: None to a lot
Materials: A piece of 8.5 x 11-inch white paper for each child, washable markers in many colors, and scissors

Game: Give each child a piece of 8.5 x 11-inch white paper and some markers. Ask the children to draw an outline of their name on the paper (as large as possible). Then have the children color in their letters and decorate their sheets.

When they finish, ask them to hand in their papers. Mix up the papers so that the children cannot see them. If you have five children or fewer present, have the group work together. Otherwise, form groups of three to four children.

Have the children take turns saying their names aloud and saying something about their pet or favorite animal. As children talk, cut up the name papers into puzzle pieces. Cut about eight pieces per sheet. Mix up the pieces and keep them together. Only cut up the sheets that you need. For example, if you have three groups, make three puzzles from the colored-name papers.

Give each group the pieces to one of the names. (Make sure each group has all the pieces.) Say, "The Bible talks about secrets and mysteries. We know about those secrets because they're about the Christ we follow. Now we're going to solve our own mysteries. Each group has a puzzle. I want you to put your puzzle together and figure out whose name it says. Once you figure it out, keep quiet until I tell you what to do next."

Do the activity. When groups are done, have each group report on their solved mysteries. Then have the group point to the child who has that name.

End the activity by saying, "Each one of us has a beautiful name. You're good at solving puzzles and figuring out who has which name."

38

Many Links

Topic: Christian living
Scripture: 1 Thessalonians 4:1-2
Familiarity Between Children: None to a lot
Materials: Lots of paper clips

39

Game: Say, "First Thessalonians tells us to live a life that pleases God. That means playing together, working hard in school, and getting to know other children. Let's play a game that helps us get to know each other more."

Form groups of three or four children. Give each group a pile of paper clips. Have the children make a paper-clip chain based on the age of all the children in the group. (For example, one group with a six- year-old, a seven-year-old, and an eight-year-old would make a paper-clip chain that is twenty-one paper clips long since 6 + 7 + 8 = 21.) If you want to make other paper-clip chains, consider these ideas:

- Number of teeth each child in the group has lost
- Number of people living in each child's home
- Number of vacations each child has taken
- Number of times each child has had the hiccups

If you wish, compare paper-clip chain lengths. Talk about what you learned about each other. You may also want to link all the paper-clip chains to make one long chain to display.

End the activity by having the children sit in a circle. Give each child one paper clip. Have the children create a paper-clip chain by naming one way to live as a Christian (such as being nice or helping others). At the end, say, "Amen."

Guess Who?

Topic: God's goodness
Scripture: Psalm 36:5-9
Familiarity Between Children: Some to a lot
Materials: An index card for each child and washable markers

Game: Give each child an index card and a marker. Say, "I want you to write your name on your index card and then one thing about you that no one knows. For example, maybe you had chicken pox when you were a baby. Maybe you moved from Alabama to Texas when you were two. Maybe you like turnip soup. Write one thing and don't let anyone see what you wrote."

Assist the children who are too young to write. Work with them individually and have them whisper what is unique about them. Write what they say on the index card.

Once the children have finished, have them fold their cards in half. Collect the cards in a pile. Say, "I'm going to give each one of you a card. If you get your own card, exchange it for another card."

Have the children take turns reading aloud what is unique on the index card without reading the child's name. Assist the children who may need help with reading. Then have the group guess who the card is about. Have the children keep guessing until the right person is guessed. Then ask the person for more details about what he or she wrote.

Do this until each child has had a turn.

End the activity by saying, "In God's goodness, God made each one of us. God loves us so much that God made us unique, wonderful people."

40

How Many Did You Take?

Topic: Christian living
Scripture: Colossians 1:10-14
Familiarity Between Children: None to a lot
Materials: A one-pound bag of M&M® candies and a bowl

41

Game: Place the M&M® candies in a bowl. Have the children sit in a circle. Pass the bowl around the circle and ask each child to take some candy but not to eat any yet.

Some children will take a lot of candy. Others will take a little. That's okay. It's all part of the game.

Once each child has taken some candy, start the game. Choose one child to start (and then move clockwise around the circle). Say, "We're going to play a get-to-know-you game. For every piece of candy that you have taken, tell us one thing about yourself." Pause. Most likely the kids who took the most candy will groan.

Start with one child. Encourage the child to start with one pile and move candy to a second pile as he or she names things. For example, if a child has ten pieces of candy, she might say: she has two cats, she likes to paint, she loves pasta, she likes playing with her best friend Sandy, she likes to read, she watches cartoons on Saturday mornings, she doesn't like going to bed, she likes to swim, she hates picking up her bedroom, and she likes knock-knock jokes. Once the child has finished, he or she can eat the candy, and you can move on to the next child.

Do this until each child has had a turn.

End the activity by reading aloud Colossians 1:10-14. Say, "God likes to know everything about us. God likes to know what we love and what we dislike. We can make good choices as Christians and still have likes and dislikes."

Spinning Good News

Topic: Compliments
Scripture: Jeremiah 33:2-3
Familiarity Between Children: Some to a lot
Materials: A bottle that spins well

42

Game: Have the children sit in a circle. Place a bottle in the middle of the circle. Ask for a volunteer. Have the volunteer spin the bottle. The child who spun the bottle must say the name of the child the bottle is pointing to and something positive about that child. It can be a compliment, a story about the child, or what he or she admires about the child. (If the bottle points to the child who spun it, the child needs to say something about him- or herself.)

Once the child has finished, have the child the bottle pointed to be the new spinner. Play again. Do this many times.

End the activity by saying, "You said all kinds of wonderful and marvelous things about each other. God also knows wonderful and marvelous things about you. The book of Jeremiah says that, and it is true. I'm glad we have so many wonderful, marvelous kids in this group."

Do You Know?

Topic: Friendships
Scripture: 1 Samuel 20:17
Familiarity Between Children: A little to a lot
Materials: None

43

Game: Have the children sit in a circle. Say, "We're going to play a guessing game. Before we play, look around the circle and secretly choose one child. Notice what color hair the child has and what he or she is wearing. If you know more things about the child, such as what he or she likes, you can also use that. Now I'm going to choose two children. The first child will tell the second child three clues about his or her secret person. Then the second child has three guesses to choose the correct child."

Slowly walk through the game one time so that the children know how it is played. Then play the game. Once a turn is finished, have the second child be the one who gives the clue while you pick another child to guess. Play the game a number of times.

End the activity by saying, "In the Old Testament, there were two best friends: Jonathan and David. They knew everything about each other, and they cared for each other very much. I'm glad to see that friendships are developing in our group. It's a lot more fun to come when we have friends."

Follow, Follow

Topic: Following, Good example
Scripture: Hebrews 6:11-12
Familiarity Between Children: None to a lot
Materials: None

Game: Read aloud Hebrews 6:11-12. Have the children stand in a circle. Teach them this chant:

> Can you do what (_Name of Child_) does?
> Yes, we can. Yes, we can.
> Tell us, (_Name of Child_), what to do.
> Here we go. Here we go.

Once the children know the chant, explain that you will choose one child to lead the group. Everyone will say that child's name at the beginning of the chant, and then the child will demonstrate a movement for everyone to do during the "Here we go. Here we go" part of the chant.

The leading child can wiggle, jump up and down, twirl around, clap and kick, or do whatever motion that child chooses. Everyone else follows.

Once one child has done the motion, do the chant again with another child's name. Do this until each child has had a turn.

End the activity by saying, "You all did a great job of choosing fun motions and following each other. God likes it when we follow the good example of others."

44

From Here to There

Topic: Trust
Scripture: Deuteronomy 8:2-4
Familiarity Between Children: None to a lot
Materials: A large playing area

45

Game: Briefly tell the story of the Israelites from Deuteronomy 8:2-4. Explain that God is always with us wherever we go.

Designate three areas of the room. Choose an area to the far left, to the far right, and one in the middle, Make sure the children know where these three areas are.

Say, "I'm going to name different things. Whatever fits you best, run to that area." Start by naming hair color. Say, "Everyone with black hair, run to the far right. Everyone with brown hair, run to the middle. Everyone with blonde hair, run to the far left." Have the children do this. Once they get to their places, have each group form a circle and take turns saying their first names to each other. Explain that they will do this after every statement you read.

Read statements such as these:

- If you like to swim best, run to the far right. If you like to run best, run to the far left. If you would rather sit on the couch, run to the middle.
- If you like TV best, run to the far right. If you like computers best, run to the far left. If you would rather play video games, run to the middle.
- If you like milk best, run to the far right. If you like juice best, run to the far left. If you would rather drink water, run to the middle.

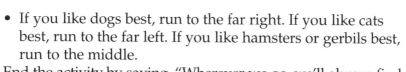

- If you like dogs best, run to the far right. If you like cats best, run to the far left. If you like hamsters or gerbils best, run to the middle.

End the activity by saying, "Wherever we go, we'll always find other people with us. Wherever we go, we'll always find God."

Name Chase

Topic: Names
Scripture: 3 John 14-15
Familiarity Between Children: Some to a lot
Materials: None

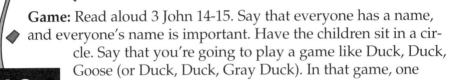

Game: Read aloud 3 John 14-15. Say that everyone has a name, and everyone's name is important. Have the children sit in a circle. Say that you're going to play a game like Duck, Duck, Goose (or Duck, Duck, Gray Duck). In that game, one

child walks around the circle and pats each child's head while saying, "Duck." When the child patting children's heads says either "Goose" or "Gray Duck" the child whose head was tapped jumps up and chases the other child around the circle. If the second child catches the running child before making it around the circle, he or she gets to sit down. If he or she does not, the first child can sit down in the "Goose" or "Gray Duck" place while the other child then starts around the circle saying, "Duck."

Explain that you're going to play a slightly different version of this game. The only difference is that the child walking around the circle patting children's heads will name each child by his or her first name and then say, "chase" to the child who will then jump up and chase the other child around the circle. For example, the game could sound like, "Henry, Michelle, Haley, Katelyn, Xavier, Jacob, chase" before the child starts to run. (If you happen to have a child present whose name is Chase, have the children say *run* instead of *chase*.)

Play this game a number of times.

End the activity by walking around the circle and patting each child's head while saying his or her first name. Then say, "God loves each one of you, and God knows you each by name."

Partner Scavenger Hunt

Topic: Working together
Scripture: Exodus 31:12-17
Familiarity Between Children: None to some
Materials: Cloth strips to tie together pairs of children for a three-legged race, lunch-size paper bags, and a bunch of pennies, stones, crayons, paper clips, and cotton balls

Game: Before you play this game, hide pennies, stones, crayons, paper clips, and cotton balls throughout the room. Make sure the children are not present when you hide these items. If you don't

have time to hide items before the lesson, have another volunteer take the children out of the room to explore another part of your church while you hide the items.

Once everything is hidden, create teams of two. Pair children together who don't know each other well. If you have an extra child, have that child team up with an adult. Have pairs stand side by side and tie their middle legs together, like they're going to participate in a three-legged race. Give each pair a lunch-size paper bag. Have partners introduce themselves to each other.

Say, "Around the room are a bunch of things that are hidden. I want you to find five different items, and only one of each item. I would like you to find one penny, one stone, one crayon, one paper clip, and one cotton ball. Work together to move around the room, pick up these items, and place them in your bag. When you're finished, take a seat and talk about the things you like to do so that you and your partner can get to know each other better."

Play the game. When the children finish, end the game by saying, "A scavenger hunt is always easier when you're by yourself because you can make all the decisions, but a scavenger hunt with other people is more fun because you get to know the other person. In Exodus 31, the people worked together, just like you did today. Now it's time for us to rest." Untie the children's legs and move on to another part of your lesson.

Alphabet Pop-up

Topic: God's love
Scripture: 1 John 3:1
Familiarity Between Children: None to a lot
Materials: None

Game: Read aloud 1 John 3:1. Have the children gather in a large, open area and squat down. Say, "We're going to pop like popcorn. I'm going to say a letter of the alphabet. If your first or last name begins with that letter, pop up by jumping up, say aloud either your first or last name that starts with that letter, and then squat back down."

Do a practice pop up before you begin. Then go in order of the alphabet from A to Z, pausing between each letter so that children can pop up. For example, when you say A, children may pop up and say, "Alan," "Abby," and "Anderson."

Once you finish the alphabet, consider playing the game again, but have the children pop up and name things they're glad God created that start with each letter. For example, you might hear "Animals" and "Apples" when you say the letter A.

End the game by saying, "From A to Z, God loves each one of you."

Frozen Name Tag

Topic: Names
Scripture: John 10:1-5
Familiarity Between Children: Some to a lot
Materials: None

49

Game: Read aloud John 10:1-5. Talk about how shepherds know the names of each one of their sheep. Ask the children for the names of their pets. Then say that God knows the names of every animal and every person.

Say you're going to play a game based on Frozen Tag. One person will be *IT*. The difference is that when *IT* tags you, he or she must also say your correct first name at the same time as tagging you. Then you must freeze. No one can unfreeze you. Once you're frozen, stay frozen in position.

Explain that if *IT* tags you and calls you by a name that isn't your name, you can keep running, but you must say, "That's not my name. My name is (*and say your name*)."

Play the game. If you have a lot of kids, consider having two or three children be *IT* at the same time. Once about half of the children are frozen into place, stop the game and choose another child to be *IT*.

End the game by saying, "When we know each other's names, we can have a lot of fun together. Now let's have more fun together by going on to the next thing in our lesson."

Crazy Hair

Topic: Joy, laughter
Scripture: Deuteronomy 16:14-15
Familiarity Between Children: None to a lot
Materials: An index card for each child, washable markers, and lots of hair accessories: ponytail holders, barrettes, hair clips, hairnets, and anything else you can put in your hair

Game: Give each child an index card. Have each child write his or her name on the card. (Assist the younger children in doing this.) Collect all the cards. Shuffle them and put them in a pile. Have the children sit in a circle. Read aloud Deuteronomy 16:14-15. Say that there are times when we can laugh and have fun, and this is one of those times.

Place all the hair accessories in the middle of the circle. Say, "We're going to take turns going around the circle. Choose one card from the pile that I hand you. It will be one of our names. If you know the child whose name is on the card, pick a hair accessory from the middle of the circle and place it in that child's hair. If you don't know the child or have trouble reading the name, ask me and I'll help you. Then choose a hair accessory and place it in that child's hair."

Play the game. Once each child has chosen a name from the index cards, have the child place the card back into the pile toward the bottom. Then give the next child in the circle the stack of index cards. Go around the circle a number of times so that the children have three or four items in their hair.

End the game by saying, "We all look silly with our crazy hair. Let's all make a crazy face to match our crazy hair." (*Pause so that the children can do this.*) Say, "Thank you, God, for silly times like this."

Part 3

Great Games for OLDER CHILDREN

W hat's delightful about fourth- to sixth-graders is that they're able to do so much more than younger children. They're adept at writing, drawing, and playing together. They're being challenged academically at school, and they're more likely to engage in Christian education if you challenge them intellectually, socially, and physically. That's why games are so essential for this age group.

Unfortunately, this is the age when a number of kids resist coming to church. Building community among fourth- to sixth-graders is most effective when you understand the many changes kids are going through and you work *with* those changes instead of *against* them. Between the ages of ten and twelve, children experience rapid changes that affect how they interact with each other. Around the ages of ten to eleven, girls and boys tend to separate more by gender. Thus, for kids who had a close relationship with a friend of the opposite sex, this change can feel quite personal and devastating. The more children understand that they're changing and that friendships often change along with that, the more they can settle into your group.

Boys tend to be more flexible than girls. If a boy's best friend isn't around, he often will seek out another boy to play with. Girls, on the other hand, can be cliquey at this age. Their relationships are often full of drama. Two girls may gang up on a third. Jealousy may rear its head, and if you don't keep an eye out for it, you can very easily have kids picking on each other or intentionally leaving someone out.

Although some children can be mean at this age, usually the ones that pick on others are the ones who are most self-conscious. They have been hurt, and they're working hard not to get hurt again. Show them better ways to interact with others, and help kids get to know each other. Play games to help expand their circles of friendships. If you have strong cliques, separate the kids in the clique and pair them up with kids they don't know well. Make sure everyone is included.

Since fourth- to sixth-graders are heading to the teenage years, it's critical that they feel welcome and that they belong. Whenever children enter your classroom, greet each one by name. Smile and look into their eyes. Tell them how happy you are to see them. During your time together, make a lot of eye contact. Point out what kids are doing right, and have fun together. When it's time to leave, call them by name again. Tell them that you can't wait to see them next time. Fourth- to sixth-graders will keep coming back as long as they know they belong. Do whatever you can to show that each one is important.

Everybody Counts

Topic: Name
Scripture: Ecclesiastes 7:1
Familiarity Between Children: A little to a lot
Materials: A die (or create a large die out of a 4-inch by 4-inch white gift box by drawing dots on each side with a black permanent marker), and a beanbag

Game: Say, "Ecclesiastes 7:1 says that a good name is invaluable. Let's see how well you know each other's name by playing this game."

Have the children sit in a circle. Go around the circle and have each child say his or her first name. Give one child the die and have the child roll it. (The child will get a number between one and six.) Give that child the beanbag. Explain that the child will need to point to the number of children on the die (for example three), say each child's name correctly, and then gently toss the beanbag to the third child. (If the child rolls a six on the die, he or she would have to name six children correctly and then throw the beanbag to the sixth child.)

Once the child has finished his or her turn, the child who was tossed the beanbag gets to throw the die to see how many children he or she must name. If a child misnames a child, ask for a volunteer to name the child correctly. (The goal is for children to learn each other's names not to compete to see who does—or does not—know children's names.)

If most children know each other's name, use a timer. See if the children can name children (by the number on the die) within ten seconds or less. Go faster and faster as the children become adept at knowing each other's names.

End the game by saying, "Everyone counts. Each one of you is an important child of God."

Your Opinion Matters

Topic: Opinions
Scripture: Luke 10:25-37
Familiarity Between Children: Some to a lot
Materials: A chair for each child

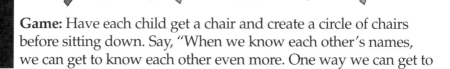

52

Game: Have each child get a chair and create a circle of chairs before sitting down. Say, "When we know each other's names, we can get to know each other even more. One way we can get to know each other is by hearing the different opinions we have."

Ask the children what an opinion is. Emphasize that one opinion is not better than another. Opinions grow out of our beliefs and values. Explain that hearing people articulate their opinions helps us form our own opinions.

Say, "Luke 10:25-37 tells the story of the good Samaritan." Read aloud the scripture passage or ask a child to read it. Explain that you're going to name different kinds of people and children should stand if they believe the answer is yes, that person is a neighbor and should be helped, or they should stay sitting if the answer is no, the person is not a neighbor and should not be helped. After you name a type of person, have one child who said yes explain why he or she has that opinion. Then have a child who said no tell his or her idea. After the pro and con explanations, have all the children sit before you name a different type of person.

Name people, such as these:

- People in your neighborhood
- Bullies
- People of different races
- Terrorists
- Murderers
- People in your family
- Friends
- Enemies
- People who hurt you
- Mean people
- Poor people
- Rich people
- People with disabilities

End the game by saying, "Your opinion matters. It's important to think about what you believe in and to form opinions. God loves us—no matter what kind of opinion we have."

The Beauty of a Name

Topic: Name, self-esteem
Scripture: Esther 1:11
Familiarity Between Children: A little to a lot
Materials: A piece of 8.5 x 11-inch white paper for each child, markers in many colors, and blue painter's tape

Game: Give each child a piece of 8.5 x 11-inch white paper and some markers. Ask the children to draw an outline of their name on the paper (as large as possible). Then have the children fill in the letters with pictures of what they like, such as certain animals, a school subject, a musical instrument, a sport, what a perfect day looks like, and so on.

Once the children have finished, ask them to take turns standing up. Have each child first say his or her name and then describe the pictures drawn. After, ask the rest of the group if they have any questions.

Do this until each child has had a turn.

End the activity by saying, "In the book of Esther, King Xerxes thought the queen was beautiful. He wanted the queen to wear her crown and show what made her beautiful to all the guests. Each one of us is a queen or a king in our own way. Our names and our interests make us beautiful."

Julie Says; Jose Says

Topic: Jesus, following Jesus
Scripture: Mark 2:13-14
Familiarity Between Children: None to a lot
Materials: None

Game: Say, "In Mark 2, Jesus called people to follow him. It was a lot like the game of Simon Says, except that it was Jesus who was doing the saying."

Explain that you're going to play Simon Says, except that the person who is *IT* will use his or her name. For example, if Julie is *IT*, she will say, "Julie says." If Jose is *IT*, he will say, "Jose says."

Choose one person to be *IT*. Have that person stand in front of the group, facing the group. Remind the children that when the person uses his or her name, they should follow the command. If the person doesn't use his or her name, they need to remain still. Encourage the person who is *IT* to act out the command, whether or not he or she says his or her name. It's harder not to follow a verbal command when someone is doing the action.

Play the game. Let up to three children have a turn at being *IT*.

End the game by saying, "(_Say Your Name_) says it's time to get back to our lesson. (_Say Your Name_) says to gather together over here.

Favorite Saints

Topic: Saints, Bible characters
Scripture: Luke 9:28-36
Familiarity Between Children: None to a lot
Materials: An index card for each person, something to write with for each person

Game: Say, "In Luke 9, Jesus took Peter, John, and James to a hill to pray. While Jesus was praying, his clothes became white and his face glowed. Suddenly Moses and Elijah were with Jesus, even though Moses and Elijah had been dead for a long, long time. The Bible is filled with interesting people. On your index card, first write your name. Then write the name of your favorite person in the Bible."

Give the children time to do this. Once they finish, have them walk around the room and show their cards to other children, one at a time. If they find someone who has the same favorite person in the Bible, they should add that child's name to the bottom of their card and the other child will add their name to his or her card. Encourage the children to talk with each person in the group to find out who her or his favorite Bible character is.

Once you think the children have talked with all the other children, stop the activity. Ask, "Who is the most popular favorite Bible person in this room?" See what the children say. Then have the children list each of the favorite Bible people in order of popularity, with one child saying why he or she likes that person.

End the game by saying, "The Bible is filled with amazing people who followed God. We, too, can follow God and set good examples for others to follow."

Around We Go

Topic: Self-esteem
Scripture: Zephaniah 3:17
Familiarity Between Children: A little to a lot
Materials: None

Game: Have the children stand in a circle. Ask for one volunteer to stand in the center of the circle. Read aloud Zephaniah 3:17. Talk about how God delights in what we do.

Say, "We're going to play a game. The child in the middle will hold out his finger toward someone. When I say go, walk to the right as a circle. When I say stop, stop. The child in the middle will spin around and point to someone. Whoever that child points to, that child should say his or her first name and an action verb that starts with the same letter as his or her first name. For example, George giggles or Karen kicks. Then everyone repeats the phrase 'George giggles' and does the action."

If the children have a hard time thinking of action verbs that begin with the same letter as their name, use this list for ideas:

A—argue	N—nod
B—bend, burp, bounce	O—outrun
C—clap, creep	P—pray, pat
D—dance	Q—quote
E—eat	R—run
F—fly (hands out)	S—skip, sing
G—giggle, gargle	T—tiptoe
H—hop, hiccup	U—unbutton
I—inflate	V—vacate
J—jump	W—wiggle
K—kick	X—x-ray
L—leap, laugh	Y—yell, yodel
M—march	Z—zoom, zigzag

Play the game a number of times. If you wish, change the game slightly so that the child in the middle points to two people. The first one must name the second one's name and name an action.

End the game by saying, "As a group, let's gallop back to the table for the rest of our lesson."

Map It Out

Topic: Home
Scripture: Ruth 1
Familiarity Between Children: A little to a lot
Materials: A map showing the area where children from your church live (this may be a community map, a regional suburban map, a city map, or a map showing the rural communities in your area of the state), blue painter's tape, washable markers

Game: Hang up a map on the wall. Say, "In the Old Testament, Ruth said she would go with her mother-in-law, Naomi,

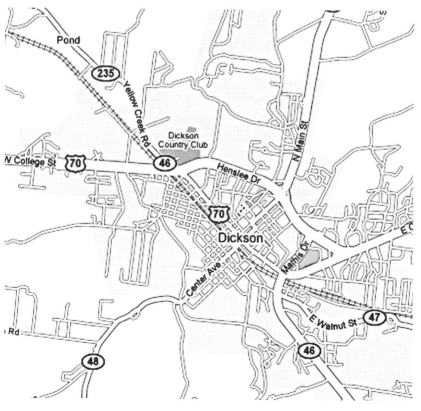

wherever Naomi would go. They were good friends, and they knew where they came from, where they lived, and where they were going."

Show the children the map. Ask if anyone can find where your church is located. Once someone has found the correct location, have someone put a star in that place with a marker.

Then one at a time, ask each child to locate where he or she lives on the map. (If your map doesn't include the location, mark the approximate location outside the map in the correct direction.) Have each child mark where he or she lives. (If you feel comfortable doing so, add where you live.)

When the map is marked, ask the group these questions:
- Who lives the closest to our church?
- Who lives the farthest from our church?
- Of all the children's homes on this map, who lives the closest to each other?
- Of all the children's homes on this map, who lives the farthest from each other?
- Who lives in the same areas?
- Who has recently moved? (Where did that person live before?)
- Who has lived in the same home their whole life?
- What has surprised you about learning where we live?

End the activity by saying, "It matters where we live. In the book of Ruth, the family lived in Moab and then moved to Bethlehem. Some of us have lived in the same home our whole lives. Some of us have recently moved. God keeps track of us no matter where we are."

Link and Learn

Topic: Names
Scripture: John 10:1-5
Familiarity Between Children: None to a lot
Materials: A chair for each child set in a circle

Game: Set up the chairs in a circle. Have each child sit in one of the chairs. As the leader, stand in the middle of the circle. Say, "In John 10, Jesus tells a parable about the shepherd knowing the name of each sheep. At church, it's good for us to know each other's names."

Go around the circle and have each child say his or her name out loud. If the children don't know each other well, say that this game will help them begin to learn each other's names.

Explain that you're going to say the name of one child. That child then needs to name two children in the circle correctly. As soon as he or she does, all four people (the person in the middle, the person named by the person in the middle of the circle, and the two children named) need to jump up and sit on another chair. (Four people will be vying for three chairs, and everyone must move. Whoever doesn't get a chair, gets to be in the middle and name the next child.) Explain that every once in a while, the person in the middle can yell out, "Everybody move!" Then everyone must move to a different chair.

Play the game.

End the game by saying, "It's fun to link and learn each other's names. The more we know each other, the more fun we'll have together."

What We Love

Topic: Love
Scripture: 1 John 4:7-12
Familiarity Between Children: A little to a lot
Materials: A piece of 8.5 x 11-inch white paper for each child, a marker for each child

1. Reading
2. Singing
3. Running
4.
5.

Game: Give each child a piece of 8.5 x 11-inch white paper and a marker. Ask the children to write their names on the top of the paper and number their paper from one to ten. Have the children write ten things they love to do. Examples could include play basketball, read, play video games, eat, sing, and so on.

Once the children have finished, ask each child to find a partner. (If you have an odd number of children, consider playing the game with the children so that everyone can always have a partner.) Encourage the children to compare lists. They should make a mark next to every item that they have in common with their partner.

Then yell, "Switch!" Children should then find another partner to compare lists.

Continue the activity until the children have worked one-on-one with each child.

End the activity by saying, "It's good to love doing different things, but what's more important is that we love each other. First John 4:7 (GNT) says, 'Dear friends, let us love one another because love comes from God. Whoever loves is a child of God and knows God'."

Groups of Friends

Topic: Friendship
Scripture: Proverbs 17:17
Familiarity Between Children: None to a lot
Materials: Pieces of paper with one letter per paper spelling the word FRIENDS (if you have a group of more than six children present, create more sets of these papers so that about every six children can form one group and have its own set of papers spelling FRIENDS

Game: Mix up the letters so that the children cannot easily figure out what the word spells. Have the children work together to spell one word using all the letters. Once a group finishes, have the children go around the circle and say his or her name aloud.

End the activity by saying, "Proverbs 17:17 says friends always show their love. We can show our love for each other by learning each other's names and also by helping each other."

Question Bounce

Topic: Questions
Scripture: 1 Samuel 20
Familiarity Between Children: Some to a lot
Materials: A chair for each child and for yourself, a ball that
will bounce (such as a bouncy ball, Ping-Pong ball,
basketball, or other type of ball)

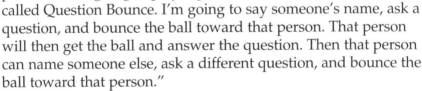

61

Game: Form a circle with the chairs.
Have everyone sit in a chair. Say,
"First Samuel 20 talks about the
close friendship between Jonathan
and David. How do we become
good friends with someone?"
Encourage the children to give their
ideas. Then say, "One way we become
better friends is by asking questions.
We find out as much as we can about a
person. We're going to play a game
called Question Bounce. I'm going to say someone's name, ask a
question, and bounce the ball toward that person. That person
will then get the ball and answer the question. Then that person
can name someone else, ask a different question, and bounce the
ball toward that person."

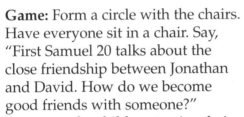

Questions could include:
* What is your favorite sport?
* Who is in your family?
* What makes you excited?
* Why do you come to this church?

Monitor the children's questions to ensure they're appropriate.
Play the game for a while.

End the game by saying, "I'm happy to know more about each
one of you. The more we learn about each other, the more we
become friends."

Trust Walk

Topic: Trust
Scripture: Psalm 119:41-48
Familiarity Between Children: Some to a lot
Materials: Two to six grocery-size paper bags, an obstacle
         course made up of chairs and other items to
         maneuver around

Game: Say, "The Bible says it is good to trust God and to trust in God's word. Since each one of us is God's people, we're going to see how well we trust each other."

If you have eight children or fewer, form one obstacle course with chairs, tables, and other items to maneuver around. If you have nine to sixteen children, form two obstacle courses side by side. If you have more than sixteen kids, form three obstacle courses side by side.

If you have eight children or fewer, have the children form a line. Give every other child in line a grocery-size paper bag. If you have nine to sixteen children, form two lines. Give the first person in each line a grocery-size paper bag. If you have more than sixteen children, from three lines and give the first person in a line a bag. Children will do this activity in pairs within their line.

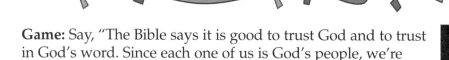

Say, "You're going to work in pairs. Say your name to your partner and have one person put the grocery-size paper bag over his or her head. The other partner will hold the 'blind' child's hand and lead the person through the obstacle course. The point is to do this safely yet quickly. When you return to the line, yell out both of your names and then the next pair can go."

Do this until each pair has had a turn. Ask the children if they want to play again with the other partner wearing the bag.

End the activity by saying, "It's hard to trust when you can't see, but God is like our partner. God is with us and leads the way."

Big Hearts

Topic: Love, friendship
Scripture: 1 Peter 4:8-10
Familiarity Between Children: Some to a lot
Materials: A piece of 8.5 x 11-inch white paper for each child, blue painter's tape, a washable marker for each child

63

Game: Give each child a piece of 8.5 x 11-inch white paper and a marker. Ask the children to draw an outline of a heart on the paper (as large as possible). Then have the children write their names at the top of the heart.

Ask the children to help each other tape their hearts to their backs. For example, Keisha will have a heart on her back that says *Keisha*.

Once the children have finished, ask each child to hold a washable marker. Say, "When I tell you to start, I want you to move around the room and write one thing you admire about each person. Write what you admire on his or her back on the heart. Be careful so that the marker only writes on the paper, not on anyone's clothes."

Do the activity.

End the activity by saying, "First Peter says it's good to love each other. Let's help each other take our hearts off our backs. Read what other people in this room love about you."

Whistling and Humming

Topic: Praise God
Scripture: Psalm 150
Familiarity Between Children: None to a lot
Materials: Slips of paper with the names of familiar songs. With ten children or fewer, make five slips of one familiar tune and five slips of another. With eleven to twenty-one children, make seven slips of one familiar tune, seven of another, and seven of a third song. If you have more than twenty-one, choose four songs. Mix up the slips of paper so that a different song appears on each one.

Game: Before you play this game, determine how many children you have. If you have ten children or fewer, choose two songs. If you have eleven to twenty-one, choose three songs. If you have

more than twenty-one, choose four songs. Choose songs that children are very familiar with, such as "Jesus Loves Me This I Know" and "Amazing Grace."

Give each child a slip of paper. Tell them not to show anyone what they have. If someone doesn't know the tune, exchange with another child. Once all the children have received their slips, have them return the slips to you. Have them spread out around the room.

Say, "The Bible says to make a joyful noise to the Lord. When I tell you to go, I want you to either hum or whistle the tune you were given on a slip of paper. Listen closely to what other people are humming and whistling. Find all the people who are whistling or humming the same tune. Let's see which group can form first."

Do the activity. After the children have found everyone in their group, have the children each say their name aloud to their group members.

End the activity by saying, "You all made beautiful noise!

What's Great about You

Topic: Self-esteem, God's children
Scripture: 1 John 3:1-3
Familiarity Between Children: None to a lot
Materials: A piece of 8.5 x 11-inch white paper for each child, washable markers in many colors, and blue painter's tape

65

Game: Give each child a piece of 8.5 x 11-inch white paper and some markers. Ask the children to write their first name on the left side of their paper with each letter placed under the other, like this:

M
I
K
E

Ask each child to think of words that describe him or her, that start with each letter. For example:

M	—	Musical
I	—	Impatient
K	—	Keeper of secrets
E	—	Excited

Once the children have finished, ask each child to take turns showing what he or she has done. If you wish, display the names on your wall. Each week, choose two children's names. As a group, brainstorm how the group sees that person. For example, the group might see MIKE as

M	—	Magical
I	—	Intelligent
K	—	Kindhearted (or kind)
E	—	Eager

End the activity by saying, "First John says each one of us is a child of God. Each one of us is special, and each one of our names is special."

Many, Many Lands

Topic: Garden of Eden, Flood, Bethlehem
Scripture: Genesis 2, Genesis 7-8, Luke 2
Familiarity Between Children: A little to a lot
Materials: Slips of paper each with a different name on it. List these names: Adam, Eve, Noah, dove, two monkeys, Mary, Joseph, Baby Jesus

66

Game: Determine how many children you have. If you have fewer than eight, make sure you have at least two characters from each place (such as Adam and Eve from the Garden of Eden story, Noah and the dove for the flood story and Mary and Joseph for the Bethlehem story). If you have more than eight, add additional characters. For example, add one snake to the Garden of Eden story, add more animals in pairs for the flood story, and name individual animals that were present at Jesus' birth, such as one sheep, one donkey, one cow, and so on.

Mix up the slips of paper. Give each child a slip of paper. Tell them not to tell anyone what is on the sheet.

Say, "Each one of you has a slip of paper. It names a person or an animal from the Bible. Go around the room and talk with one person at a time to find out what he or she has on his or her paper. If you have something that fits like a group, such as Mary and Joseph who were together, stick together and find the rest of your group. There will be three groups all together. Once you have found everyone, figure out where these people were in the Bible."

Give the children time to do the activity. When they finish, have each group report what they learned. Have each group also name each person in the group.

End the activity by saying, "The Bible is filled with stories that have interesting people and places. These stories help us make sense of our lives and give them meaning."

Blue Ribbons

Topic: Self-esteem, gifts
Scripture: 1 Corinthians 12
Familiarity Between Children: None to a lot
Materials: A piece of 8.5 x 11-inch blue paper for each child and washable markers in many colors

67

Game: Give each child a piece of 8.5 x 11-inch blue paper and some markers. Ask the children to write their names at the top and draw an outline of a first-prize ribbon (as large as possible). Say, "First Corinthians 12 tells how God gave each one of us great gifts that make us unique. Some of us are good at music. Others at sports. Some are great readers. Others are good at talking. On your ribbon, write three things that you're good at."

Once the children have finished, ask each child to take turns standing up. Have each child first say his or her name and then tell about the two or three things he or she is good at. If a child has trouble thinking of ideas, ask the group for suggestions.

Do this until each child has had a turn.

End the activity by saying, "Each one of us is special in God's eyes. Perhaps we should give God a blue ribbon for making each one of us."

Motion Commotion

Topic: Names
Scripture: Isaiah 56:4-5
Familiarity Between Children: A little to a lot
Materials: None

MARTY 1 2 3 4 5

Game: Have the children stand up and create a circle. Read aloud Isaiah 56:4-5. Say, "Each one of you is important. You will never be forgotten."

Go around the circle slowly. Ask each child to say his or her first name aloud. Once everyone finishes, go around the circle again and have the children say their first names again and how many letters are in their first name. For example, Stephanie nine, Carlos six, Amy three, and William seven.

Once the children have finished, say, "Now we're going around the circle again. This time say your name, the number of letters in your first name, and an action that we will do. Together, we will do the action the same number of times as the letters in your name. For example, if your name is Stephanie, Stephanie might say, 'Stephanie, nine, jumping jacks.' Then we'd all do nine jumping jacks together."

Do this until each child has had a turn.

End the activity by saying, "Some of us have short names. Others of us have long names. No matter whether it's short or long, we each have a beautiful name."

Treasure Box

Topic: Friendship
Scripture: Proverbs 27:10
Familiarity Between Children: A little to a lot
Materials: A slip of paper for each child, something for each
child to write with, and a box

Game: Give each child a slip of paper and something to write with. Ask the children to write their names on the paper. Then have the children fold the paper in half and put it into the box.

Once the children have finished, have them spread throughout the room. Say, "The Bible tells us not to forget our friends. Friends are great to have, and they can help us when we're in trouble."

Explain that you're going to play a game. Say, "I'm going to pull a name out of the box and read it aloud. As soon as you hear it, rush over to the person named and put one finger on the child's shoulder."

Pull out a name and read the name aloud. All the children should surround the child whose name was read. Say, "(*Name of Child*), we are all your friends." Have the children spread throughout the room again. Have the child who was just named pull a name out of the box and read it aloud.

Do this until the box is empty.

End the activity by having the children stand in a circle. Say, "We are a big group of friends. In our friendship circle, we have . . . (*go around the circle and have each child say his or her name aloud*)."

All of Me

Topic: Creation
Scripture: Isaiah 44:1-2
Familiarity Between Children: None to a lot
Materials: A large piece of white butcher paper (about six feet long) for each child, washable markers

Game: Have each child find a partner. If an odd number of children is present, have three children work together. Give each child a piece of white butcher paper. Have the children take turns lying on their piece of paper while their partner draws an outline of them. Encourage the children to be careful to draw only on the paper, not on people's clothes or bodies.

Once the children have finished their outlines, have the children work on one body part at a time (as a group). Lead them body part by body part:

- Over the top of your head, write your name.
- In your head, write what you like to think about.
- On your hands and arms, write what you like to do and make.
- In your throat, write whether you like to talk, sing, hum, or make sound effects.
- In your heart, write what you love.
- In your feet, write the names of the places you have traveled to.

Have the children form groups of three or four and share what they have written.

End the activity by saying, "God created you and made you an amazing person. Let's thank God for our heads (*tap your head twice*), our hands (*clap twice*), our hearts (*tap your chest twice*), our feet (*tap your feet twice*), and every part of us (*tap yourself all over*)."

Birthday Timeline

Topic: Birthdays
Scripture: Genesis 40:20, Matthew 14:6, Luke 2
Familiarity Between Children: None to a lot
Materials: A piece of 8.5 x 11-inch white paper for each child, washable markers in many colors, about eight feet of yarn or string, and blue painter's tape

Game: Give each child a piece of 8.5 x 11-inch white paper and some markers. Ask the children to draw an outline of a birthday cake with candles (as large as possible). Then have the children write their names (large) on the birthday cake along with the month and date of their birth with black marker. Then have them color their cakes.

Once the children have finished, say, "The Bible tells about many people's birthdays. In Genesis 40, we read about Pharaoh's birthday. In Matthew 14, King Herod has a birthday, and Luke 2 tells about Jesus' birth."

Have each child take turns standing up and saying their name and their birthday. Do this until each child has had a turn. Then have the children work together to determine the order of all their birthdays from January 1 through December 31. Once they have determined the order, hang up a piece of yarn or string along a wall (like a timeline) and place each child's birthday cake in order from January 1 through December 31. If you wish, you can have kids create one more cake for December 25 for Jesus' birth.

End the activity by saying, "The day of our birth is a very special day. Now we know the dates of each one of our births."

Everyone Together

Topic: Names, God's children
Scripture: Romans 8:16-17
Familiarity Between Children: None to a lot
Materials: A stack of 8.5 x 11-inch white paper, washable markers in many colors, and blue painter's tape

Game: Form groups of six to eight children. If you have ten children or fewer, do this as one group.

Give each group some paper and markers. Read aloud Romans 8:16. Say, "One way that we are known as God's children is by our names. As a group, I want you to create a name acrostic that connects all of your names. You have many pieces of paper because it may take a while to figure out how your names best fit together."

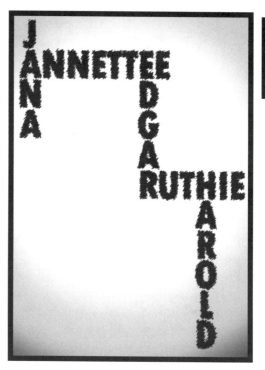

Give groups time to do the activity. If they have trouble, encourage them to start with the name that has the most letters and build from there. After they finish, have the groups show their acrostics to the other groups. Then display the acrostics on the wall.

End the activity by saying, "We are all God's children, and God loves it when we spend time together."

Group Shuffle

Topic: Disciples, groups
Scripture: Mark 3:13-19
Familiarity Between Children: None to a lot
Materials: None

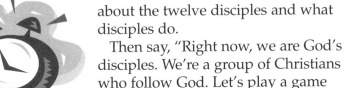

73

Game: Read aloud Mark 3:13-19. Talk about the twelve disciples and what disciples do.

Then say, "Right now, we are God's disciples. We're a group of Christians who follow God. Let's play a game called Group Shuffle."

Say that you're going to give a group a topic, and they need to make a line side by side organized by the topic. Choose one of these topics (or create one of your own):

- Your first names in alphabetical order (for example, Brian, DeAsija, Nathan, Olivia)
- From oldest to youngest (children will need to figure out their birthdays)
- From who woke up the earliest this morning to who woke up the latest
- From the quietest burper to the loudest burper (do this one only if you can tolerate some chaos and fun)
- Your last names in alphabetical order (for example, Anderson, Lopez, Quan, Young)

After the group finishes shuffling, choose another topic. Avoid topics that compare children's physical features since children are often self-conscious about their height, weight, and other aspects of themselves. Choose topics that help kids get to know each other—or get them giggling.

End the game by saying, "Our group has a bunch of wonderful kids in it. Jesus chose the twelve disciples, and Jesus also chose you to be someone special."

Favorites

Topic: Favorite things
Scripture: 1 Corinthians 7:17
Familiarity Between Children: A little to a lot
Materials: Five pieces of 8.5 x 11-inch paper, washable markers
(one for each child), and blue painter's tape

Game: Before you do this activity, label each of the five pieces
of paper. Write one label per sheet: TV show, movie, book,
sport, and music group. Then hang these five sheets around
the room on the wall with blue painter's tape.

74

Read aloud 1 Corinthians 7:17. Give each child a washable
marker. Distribute the kids evenly around the room at the five
pieces of paper. Say, "These five sheets of paper have topics,
such as TV shows, movies, and music groups. I want you to
write your favorite on each sheet. Write your favorite along with
your name. For example, if Jeremy's favorite music group is
Switchfoot, he'll write 'Switchfoot, Jeremy' on the music sheet.
When you finish writing, go clockwise to the next sheet. Write
something on each of the five sheets."

Give the children time to do this. When they finish, ask for a volunteer. Have that child choose one of the sheets and take it off the
wall. Have the child read what is written. Talk about what's on the
sheet. Try to learn more
about each child's interest
and make connections
between kids. Repeat for the
next four sheets.

End the activity by saying,
"We all have our favorites.
Sometimes we make new
friends when we find out
we have favorite things in
common."

You're Covered!

Topic: Self-esteem, friendship
Scripture: 2 Thessalonians 1:3
Familiarity Between Children: Some to a lot
Materials: Many pads of small sticky notes (about 1.5 x 2 inches), something for each child to write with

Game: Divide each pad of small sticky notes into four parts. Then have the children form small groups of their friends. (If you have a group where children don't know each other well, join that group to help them get to know each other.)

Give each child a sticky note pad and something to write with. Read aloud 2 Thessalonians 1:3. Say, "Most of you know each other quite well. When I tell you to start, I want you to write one nice thing about someone in your group and stick it on that person. When you finish, write something nice about someone else in your group and stick it on that person. Keep doing this until you're out of sticky notes. The goal is to cover the people in your group with good things that you know about them. For example, you can say that someone is nice, funny, loves chocolate, is silly, and so on. You can write only nice things though."

Begin the activity. Soon kids will be giggling and trying to cover each other with sticky notes. Some will probably try to stick them on each other's faces.

If you have a group where kids don't know each other well, do the activity slightly differently under your leadership. Ask for kids' names, where they live, who lives in their family, what they enjoy doing, and so on. Have group members write descriptive sticky notes. For example, a girl named Mariah may have sticky notes that say, Mariah, Central School, One brother, Loves popcorn, Tells jokes, Plays soccer, and so on.

Once the children have finished, ask all the kids to stand up. Say, "Look at you! You're all covered in wise words about you. Now let's all stick together." Have the group do a group hug.

Part 4

Great Games for
CHILDREN OF ALL AGES

C reating a strong community in a group of diverse ages
is critical to your children's ministry. If the children feel
connected, they'll keep coming back, and your small
group will grow closer and may even grow in number.

Unfortunately, you have a lot of dynamics to juggle with a
diverse age group. Besides the wide age span, you often have

kids from different schools and communities, and you may also have the sibling factor. Older siblings tend to want to stay far from their younger siblings, while the younger siblings tend to feel the opposite.

The keys to building a diverse community is ensuring that everyone knows each other's name and helping them form friendships. At times, you may want to break your group into smaller groups so that your younger children can get to know each other, the children in the middle-age group can get to know each other, and the older children can become familiar with one another. If this doesn't work well (for example you have one fifth grader and one sixth grader and one is a boy and one is a girl), encourage the children to bring a friend with them.

After the children get to know other children near their age, begin building connections between age groups. Create buddies where you pair an older child with a younger child. Older buddies can read picture books to their younger buddies. During Advent, have buddies go Christmas shopping together to buy presents for less fortunate children. These can be distributed through one of your community organizations.

Do whatever you can to get to know each child yourself. Often when children feel strongly connected to an adult, they gradually will feel secure enough to get to know other kids in the group. When children don't show up, make sure you reach out and let them know you missed them. Call them. E-mail them. Send them an Instant Message (IM). Drop them a note. Too many kids say that no one seems to care whether they come to church activities or not. Show them that it does matter.

Remember that your most important goal is building relationships. Children will learn more when they want to come and enjoy being with the people in your group. Pay close attention to all the relationships and dynamics in your group, and you'll see your group change for the better.

Which One?

Topic: Opinions
Scripture: Proverbs 18:4
Familiarity Between Children: None to a little
Materials: A large playing area

76

Game: Have the children stand together in front of you. Say, "We're going to get to know a little bit more about each other. I'm going to say two words or phrases. Choose the one that best fits you and move to the area of the room that represents that word or phrase." For example, say, "Which word describes you more: liking morning more (point to one end of the room) or liking evening more (point to the opposite side of the room)." Have the children move to either one end of the room (if they like morning more) or the other end of the room (if they like evening more). Then have all the morning children say their

names aloud one at a time. When they finish, have the evening children take turns saying their names aloud.

Say other words and phrases, such as these:

- Is quiet . . . or . . . Is talkative
- Likes a clean room . . . or . . . Likes a messy room
- Likes to argue . . . or . . . Likes to agree
- Likes to wear shoes . . . or . . . Likes to go barefoot
- Likes to cook food . . . or . . . Likes to eat food
- Likes to play games . . . or . . . Likes to read books
- Likes to tell jokes . . . or . . . Likes to hear jokes
- Plays outside . . . or . . . Plays inside
- Makes fast decisions . . . or . . . Likes to think before deciding
- Builds (blocks, Legos®) . . . or . . . Creates (paints, draws)
- Likes baths . . . or . . . Likes showers
- Doesn't have a pet . . . or . . . Has a pet (have children say what their pet is)

End the game by saying, "Is in this class," and pointing to one side of the room so that all the children go there. Then say, "I'm so glad each one of you is in this class. Proverbs 18:4 says, 'A person's words can be a source of wisdom, deep as the ocean, fresh as a flowing stream.' By telling us about yourselves, you're helping us get to know you."

What I Like – What I Dislike

Topic: Preferences, choices
Scripture: Matthew 3
Familiarity Between Children: A little to a lot
Materials: A piece of paper for each child, something for each child to write with, and a box

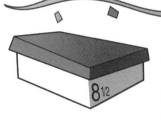

Game: Have each older child pair up with a younger child. (Ideally, match up a child who can write with a child who isn't old enough to write.) Give each child a piece of paper and something to write with. Say, "We're going to play a game about likes and dislikes. I want each of you to write your name on the top of the paper followed by three things you like and three things you dislike. Either you can write on the paper or your partner can. But don't let anyone else hear or see what is on your sheet."

Give partners time to do this. When the children finish, ask them to fold the paper in half and place it in a box. Then have partners take turns choosing a paper, reading the lists aloud (without revealing the child's name), and having the children guess who the person is.

Once the children have finished, ask them what surprised them.

End the activity by saying, "John the Baptist had strong likes and dislikes. He liked wearing clothes made from camel's hair. He ate locusts and wild honey. He baptized people. But he didn't like sin and people who wouldn't give up their sins. He disliked Pharisees and called them snakes. All of us have likes and dislikes. As we get to know each other more, we learn what makes each one of us unique."

Ready, Set, Go!

Topic: Names
Scripture: Mark 5:9
Familiarity Between Children: A little to a lot
Materials: None

78

Game: Have the children form two groups. Have one group stand side by side at one end of the room. Have the other group stand in a single line at the other end of the room. Say, "In Mark 5:9, Jesus asked someone to tell his name. Now we're going to play a name game."

Explain that children in the single line will take turns running up to the other line and naming children from left to right. If the child doesn't know a child's name, he or she can ask but then has to run back to take a place at the end of the single line. If the child can name every child in the side-by-side line correctly, that child takes a place at the far right of the side-by-side line and the child at the far left of the side-by-side line runs to take a place at the end of the single line. Then the next child at the front of the single line runs up to the side-by-side line and tries to name each child from left to right.

Slowly walk this game through first so that the children are clear about how it works. (It can seem complex at first, but once the children get the hang of it, the game will really move.) Play the game. As the children get better at knowing names, have them move faster.

End the game by saying, "Whenever we don't know someone's name, it's always good to ask. Jesus knows each one of us by name, and now we know one another's names."

Kind Compliments

Topic: Kindness, self-esteem
Scripture: Nehemiah 9:17b
Familiarity Between Children: Some to a lot
Materials: A piece of paper for each child, something for each child to write with, and a box

Game: Have each older child pair up with a younger child. (Ideally, match up a child who can write with a child who isn't old enough to write.) Give each child a piece of paper and something to write with. Say, "We're going to play a game about kindness and compliments. I want each of you to write your name on the top of the paper. Either you can write on the paper or your partner can. When you finish, drop the paper into this box."

Once the children have finished, have each child take one paper out of the box. Say, "I want you to write one kind thing or one compliment about the person on the sheet. After you have written something nice, write your name at the bottom of the paper. If you need help with writing, have your partner help you."

Once the children finish, have them place their papers back into the box. Then have each child choose one paper out of the box. Take turns reading only the compliment. Have the children guess who the compliment is about and then who gave the compliment. (This way you end up complimenting lots of children.)

End the activity by saying, "God is kind to all of us. God loves us, and God always has good things to say about us. Each one of you is a child of God, and you are special."

79

Ticking Time

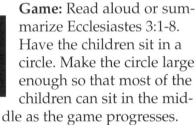

Topic: Time
Scripture: Ecclesiastes 3:1-8
Familiarity Between Children: A little to a lot
Materials: A timer that can be set to one minute and will ring
when it goes off

Game: Read aloud or summarize Ecclesiastes 3:1-8. Have the children sit in a circle. Make the circle large enough so that most of the children can sit in the middle as the game progresses.

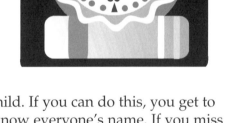

Say, "We're going to play a game about time. I'm going to set this timer for one minute, and then we'll start passing it quickly around the circle. Whoever is holding the timer when it goes off must stand up and go around the circle, saying the first name of each child. If you can do this, you get to sit in the middle because you know everyone's name. If you miss someone, you have to play again."

Play the game. As the children get to know each other's names, play the game faster. If children know each other's names very well, consider setting the time for a certain amount of time while a child names all the children in the circle.

Do this until only one child is left. Congratulate children on learning each other's names.

End the activity by saying, "There is a time for everything. Now I'm going to set this timer for thirty seconds, and I want you all back in your seats for the lesson by the time it goes off."

Who's Behind the Mask?

Topic: Friendship
Scripture: 1 Samuel 20
Familiarity Between Children: Some to a lot
Materials: A mask or disguise (like plastic gag glasses that have a big nose and mustache)

Game: Have the children sit in a circle. Ask the children to go around the circle and say their names aloud.

Say, "In the Bible, there were two good friends named Jonathan and David. Someone wanted to hurt David, so Jonathan helped David hide. We're going to play a game about hiding and finding."

Ask for one child to be the volunteer. Have that child either leave the room or turn around and close his or her eyes. Choose a child to wear a disguise. Then have the volunteer return and try to guess who is wearing the disguise.

If the children know each other well, play this game by having the person wearing the disguise also hide, making it more difficult.

Once the volunteer correctly identifies the child with the disguise, ask for another volunteer. Play again for a few times.

End the game by saying, "I'm proud of you for knowing each other's names so well. Now you're doing even better group work. You're beginning to recognize who's missing and who's wearing a disguise. Only friends can do that, and you're all becoming good friends."

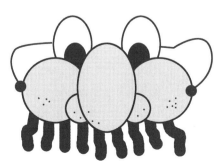

Fast Bounce

Topic: Neighbors
Scripture: Matthew 22:37-40
Familiarity Between Children: None to a lot
Materials: A ball that will bounce (such as a bouncy ball, ping pong ball, tennis ball, or other type of ball)

Game: Read aloud Matthew 22:37-40. Talk about how everyone in the room is a neighbor, even if they don't live next to each other.

Have the children form a circle. Give one child a ball. Say, "We're going to play a game called Fast Bounce. We'll start out with a topic, such as favorite colors. One person will say the name of a child across the circle and bounce the ball to that person. That person will get the ball and say his or her favorite color. Then that person will name someone else and bounce the ball to that person. Every once in a while, I'll name a different topic."

Play the game. Choose topics, such as these:

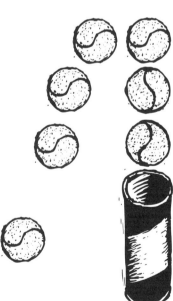

- Favorite color
- Favorite food
- Favorite sport
- Favorite book
- The job you want to have when you grow up
- Which country you'd like to visit most
- Favorite beverage
- Favorite cartoon or comic strip

End the game by saying, "When we get to know our neighbors, we have more fun with them. Now let's bounce back to our lesson."

Resident Star

Topic: Hide and seek
Scripture: Colossians 4:5-6
Familiarity Between Children: None to a lot
Materials: None

Game: Read aloud Colossians 4:5-6. Say, "It's good to be nice to each other and to treat one another with respect." Ask for a volunteer. Have that child leave the room. Have the rest of the children spread out throughout the room. Choose one child to be the star. Say, "When the volunteer returns, he or she will be looking for the star. Do not say who this person is. When the volunteer gets slightly close to the star, clap quietly. As the volunteer goes away from the star, stop clapping. If the volunteer gets closer to the star, clap more loudly."

Invite the volunteer into the room. Explain what the clapping signal means and that he or she needs to guess who is the star. Have the volunteer wander around the room. When the volunteer correctly identifies the star, have the star say his or her name aloud. Then have the star leave the room as the next volunteer. Choose a new star.

Play the game a number of times.

End the game by having the children stand in a circle. Say, "We're now going to clap for each other. Let's go around the circle and say each of our names aloud, and clap after every name."

83

Jump Up

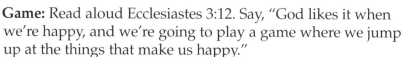

Topic: Happiness
Scripture: Ecclesiastes 3:12
Familiarity Between Children: None to a lot
Materials: None

Game: Read aloud Ecclesiastes 3:12. Say, "God likes it when we're happy, and we're going to play a game where we jump up at the things that make us happy."

Have the children spread throughout the room. Have them get into a squatting position. Explain that you're going to read different statements. If you name something that makes them happy, children are to jump up, say their names aloud, and remain standing. When you're ready to read another statement, have the children squat down again. (If only a few children stand for certain statements, point this out to the group.)

Read aloud statements, such as these:

- Likes macaroni and cheese
- Plays a musical instrument (then ask each standing child for the instrument's name)
- Loves computers
- Plays a sport (then ask each standing child for the name of the sport)
- Likes dogs better than cats
- Has a teacher who is a man
- Likes liver
- Likes to read
- Likes to play

End the game by saying, "Different things make each one of us happy. The Bible says it is good to be happy."

Human Tic-tac-toe

Topic: Moses
Scripture: Exodus chapters 2–4
Familiarity Between Children: None to a lot
Materials: Four Bibles, a piece of 8.5 by 11-inch white paper for
each child, washable markers, blue painter's tape,
and a coin

Game: Give each child a piece of 8.5 x 11-inch white paper.
Ask the children to each write their first name on top of the
piece of paper. Then divide the group in half. (Make sure you

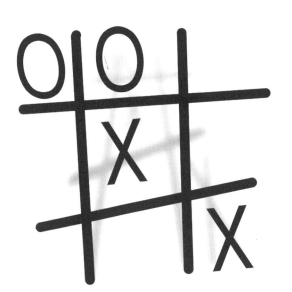

have a good
mix of older
and younger
children in each
group.) Have
half of the chil-
dren draw a
large X under
their name on
the paper. Have
the other half
draw a large O
under their
name on the
paper. Have all
the children
with Os sit
together and all

the children with Xs sit together. Give each group two Bibles.
   Make a tic-tac-toe grid on the floor with blue painter's tape.
Make the grid large enough so that there is room inside each
square for a person to stand.

Explain that you're going to play a game of human tic-tac-toe. Have children open the Bibles to Exodus chapters 2–4. Say that you're going to play a game about Moses, and the answers are in chapters 2–4. Flip a coin to see which group will go first. Ask that group a question. If someone from the group answers it correctly, that person gets to choose a square on the tic-tac-toe grid to stand in. Then go to the next team and ask another question. If someone gets an answer wrong, the other team gets a chance to answer the question.

Ask questions, such as these:

- Where was Moses placed as a baby to save his life? (*Answer: In a basket in the river, Exodus 2:3*)
- Who found the basket? (*Answer: The king's daughter, Exodus 2:5*)
- Who raised baby Moses for the princess? (*Answer: Moses' real mom, a Hebrew, Exodus 2:8-9*)
- Who was Moses's father-in-law? (*Answer: Jethro, Exodus 3:1*)
- How did God talk to Moses? (*Answer: Through a burning bush, Exodus 3:2-3*)
- What did God want Moses to take off near the burning bush? (*Answer: His sandals or shoes, Exodus 3:5*)
- Why did God want Moses to remove his sandals? (*Answer: Moses was standing on holy ground, Exodus 3:5*)
- Who did God want Moses to save? (*Answer: The Israelites, Exodus 3:9*)
- From whom? (*Answer: The Egyptians, Exodus 3:7-10*)
- Why? (*Answer: The Egyptians had enslaved the Israelites, Exodus 3:7-10*)
- What did Moses' walking stick turn into when Moses threw it on the ground? (*Answer: A snake, Exodus 4:3*)
- Why did Moses think God made a bad choice in choosing Moses to be a leader? (*Answer: Moses spoke poorly, Exodus 4:10*)
- Who did God pick to speak for Moses? (*Answer: Aaron, Exodus 4:14*)
- Who was Aaron? (*Answer: Moses' brother, Exodus 4:14*)

When one team gets tic-tac-toe, applaud the winners.

Rolling Marbles

Topic: Faith
Scripture: 1 Timothy 6:12-16
Familiarity Between Children: None to a lot
Materials: A spoon for each child, a bag of marbles, and a
        bucket

Game: Give each child a spoon. Form two groups of children. If you have six children or fewer, have them run the race twice.

Set up two lines and have the children line up in single file. Mark a destination point about six to ten feet away from the front of each group. (For example, set out a chair in front of each group for the children to walk around.) Place a bucket in the space between the two chairs.

Say, "The Bible talks about running the race of faith. We're going to play a running game. When I tell you to go, the first person in each line will walk fast or run with his or her spoon full of marbles to the chair, around the chair, and back. If the child does not drop any marbles, he or she can then carefully transfer the marbles from his or her spoon to the second person in line, who then takes off. If any marbles drop, carefully pick them up so you don't drop any more marbles. Walk quickly to the bucket, and drop in the marble(s) that fell off. Shout your name for each marble you drop into the bucket."

Give the first person marbles to carry on his or her spoon. Give each child the same amount.

Play the game.

Once the children have finished the race, say, "First Timothy says to run your best in the race, and each one of you has done that. Running while hanging on to your faith is an admirable thing to do."

Noisy Animals

Topic: Animals
Scripture: Genesis 1:20-25
Familiarity Between Children: None to a lot
Materials: A piece of 8.5 x 11-inch white paper for each child, a
washable marker for each child, and blue painter's
tape

87

Game: Give each child a piece of
paper and a marker. Ask the children
to choose an animal that makes an
interesting sound (such as a dog, cow,
or lion) and write the name of (or
draw) the animal on one side of the
paper without anyone else seeing it.
Once they finish, have each child turn
over the paper and write his or her first

name on the paper in large letters. (Older children may need to
help the younger children.)

Once the children have finished, have them tape their papers
(with their names facing forward) to the top of their legs. (Older
girls may get self-conscious with this activity if sheets are taped
to their chests.)

Say, "In Genesis, God created lots of animals. When I tell you
to go, start making your animal sound. When someone guesses it
correctly, have that child sign his or her name on your paper.
When you have everyone's name on your sheet of paper, shout
that you're done." You may want to give them the number of
total children present to know when they're done.

Play the game.

End the activity by having the children sit in a circle. Have the
children go around the circle, say their first name, and make the
noise of their animal. Say, "God created all creatures from animals to creatures like you and me."

Connecting Points

Topic: Body
Scripture: 1 Corinthians 12:12-31
Familiarity Between Children: None to a little
Materials: A nametag for each child, something to write with

Game: Give each child a nametag and something to write with. Have the children write their names on the nametags (older children may need to help younger). Have the children put their nametags on their chests.

Say, "The Bible talks about how a body has eyes, ears, arms, and so on. Every part of our body is important. We're going to play a game where I want you to pay attention to body parts and also the name of the partner you connect with. When I yell out a body part, find the person closest to you and connect the body part I called out with the body part of your partner. Look at your partner's nametag. I will then ask some people for the name of their partner."

Have the children spread out and walk around the room randomly. Periodically call out a body part, such as one of these:

- Fingers
- Ears
- Stomachs
- Noses
- Shoulders
- Feet
- Hips
- Elbows
- Knees
- Head
- Backs
- Rear ends

After the children have connected with a partner, randomly choose two or three different children (one at a time) and ask for the name of their partner. Then have the children leave their partners and mill around the room again before you call out another body part. Encourage the children to connect up with a different partner each time.

End the game by having the children form a circle. Say, "It's good that we're all connected. Now let's go arm-in-arm back to our lesson."

Skittles® Tales

Topic: Trust
Scripture: Psalm 33:20-22
Familiarity Between Children: Some to a lot
Materials: A bag of Skittles®, a bowl

Game: Have the children sit in a circle. Open a bag of Skittles® and place them in the bowl.

Read aloud Psalm 33:20-22.

Say, "God knows everything about us, and God says we can always trust God. We're going to tell something about ourselves as we pick out a piece of candy. The color you get will determine your question."

Give one child the bowl. Have that child choose a piece of candy. Ask one of the following questions (depending on the color of the candy):

- Red—What do you do when you're really mad?
- Orange—What are you most proud of?
- Yellow—How are you most like your mom (or another significant family member)?
- Green—If you could change one thing, what would it be?
- Purple—What three words would you use to describe yourself?

Allow the children to eat their piece of candy once they have answered the question. Then go to the next person and continue around the circle a number of times.

Note: This game encourages children to reveal more about themselves than other games do. Be aware that some children may reveal more than you'd hope. If that happens, encourage children not to tell other people. If you learn about something alarming, such as potential abuse, make sure you talk to a leader in your congregation who will know if you need to report anything.

End the game by saying, "All of us get mad and get hurt. We also are happy and proud about certain things. It's good to pray about every part of our lives."

Puzzlers

Topic: Confusion
Scripture: Genesis 11:1-9
Familiarity Between Children: None to a lot
Materials: Two simple toddler puzzles with about six to ten pieces each and two manila envelopes

Game: Before you do this activity, place all the puzzle pieces of one puzzle (except for one piece) into one manila envelope. Place all the puzzle pieces of the second puzzle (except for one piece) into the other manila envelope. Place the extra puzzle piece from the first puzzle into the second manila envelope, and place the extra puzzle piece from the second puzzle into the first manila envelope. (Thus each envelope will have one piece that doesn't fit.)

Tell the story about the tower of Babylon from Genesis 11:1-9. Form two groups. Have the children in each group introduce themselves by their first names.

Give each group one envelope. Encourage the groups to put their puzzles together as quickly as possible to see who will win. Watch what the children do when they discover that one of the pieces doesn't fit. See how long it takes for someone to realize that the other group has the missing puzzle piece.

End the activity by saying, "Sometimes life is confusing. We think we have all the pieces, but we don't. That's why it's helpful to look around and see what else is around us. When life gets confusing, stop and look instead of forcing something to fit."

90

Sticking Together

Topic: Fellowship, community
Scripture: 1 John 1:3
Familiarity Between Children: None to a lot
Materials: A couple of rolls of masking tape

Game: Read aloud 1 John 1:3. Say, "The Bible says it is good for Christians to stick together."

Give each child four pieces of masking tape that are about one foot long each. Have the children stick one end of the four pieces of masking tape to their arms.

Have the children mill around the room. Tell them that when you yell out the word "stick," each child should find a partner. Partners should each use one piece of masking tape to tape themselves to each other. Then have partners mill around the room together.

Yell out the word "stick." This time, partners should each find another partner and use another piece of masking tape to secure themselves to each other. Encourage the children to find ways to stick together where they can still move. Have the groups of four mill around the room.

Yell out the word "stick." This time, groups of fours should connect up with another group of four. If you have more than eight children present, do the activity one last time and have the children tape them-selves to the other groups and make one large blob. Then see how the blob moves.

End the game by say-ing, "As Christians, let's stick together, not with tape but with each other."

What's True, What's False?

Topic: Truth
Scripture: Mark 6:3
Familiarity Between Children: A little to a lot
Materials: None

Game: Have the children create a circle. Say, "We're going to play a game. I want you to think of three statements about yourself. Two need to be true and one needs to be false. When it's your turn, I want you to say all three statements. Then the rest of us will guess which one is false."

Begin the game by using Jesus as an example. "If Jesus were here, Jesus might pick these three statements for this game. See if you can figure out which one is false. The first one is that Jesus was a carpenter. The second one is that Jesus had a brother named Joseph. The third one is that Jesus didn't have any sisters."

Let the children guess. The correct answer is the third statement, that Jesus didn't have any sisters. That statement is false. Mark 6:3 says this about Jesus, "Is not this the carpenter, the son of Mary and brother of James and Joses and Judas and Simon, and are not his sisters here with us?"

Play the game with the children's statements. For example, one girl said that she liked doing Kung Fu, had been to Africa, and that she liked soccer. Most kids guessed that she hadn't been to Africa. Some guessed that she didn't like Kung Fu since she was quiet and shy. The truth was that she didn't like soccer. She had been to Africa, and she was a second-degree green belt in Kung Fu.

Play the game until everyone has had one turn. End the game by saying, "It's time to go home. FALSE. It's time to get back to our lesson. TRUE. We will all go right now. TRUE."

You Think What?

Topic: Imagination
Scripture: Ezekiel 13:1-2
Familiarity Between Children: None to a little
Materials: None

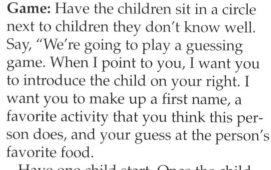

Game: Have the children sit in a circle next to children they don't know well. Say, "We're going to play a guessing game. When I point to you, I want you to introduce the child on your right. I want you to make up a first name, a favorite activity that you think this person does, and your guess at the person's favorite food.

Have one child start. Once the child finishes, have the child on the right say his or her correct first name, true favorite activity, and true favorite food. Then have that child make up a first name, a made-up favorite activity, and a guess at the person's favorite food for the child on the right. Continue around the circle until everyone has had a turn.

Say, "It's good to use our imaginations; but we need to use our imaginations in good ways, not hurtful ways. Sometimes when we don't know someone, we make up stories about him or her. Ezekiel 13:1-2 in the Bible says that this is bad. Instead, it is better to introduce yourself and get to know the person. Then together you can use your imaginations to create new worlds and stories."

End the activity by saying, "Let's walk backwards to our lesson."

Mingle and Mix

Topic: Community
Scripture: 1 John 1:5-7
Familiarity Between Children: None to a lot
Materials: None

Game: Have the children gather together. Read aloud 1 John 1:5-7, emphasizing verse seven. Say, "Let's learn more about each other through this game."

Explain that you're going to name a topic and the children need to talk with each other to figure out which group they are in for that topic. The goal is to create groups that have children with similarities.

Name topics such as these:

• Group by age
• Group by the town (or area of the city) you live in
• Group according to the number of letters in your first name (For example, Thomas, Linnea, Daniel, and Leslie would all form a group since they each have six letters in their first name.)
• Group according to school grade
• Group according to the number of pets you have

End the game by saying, "To get to know each other, we need to talk to each other and ask questions. This game helped us learn more about each other and find out what we have in common."

Card Mixer

Topic: Groups
Scripture: Acts 6:1-7
Familiarity Between Children: None to a lot
Materials: A deck of playing cards

95

Game: Give each child one playing card. Say, "In Acts 6, people began to fight with each other because they divided themselves into groups that didn't work. We're going to play a game where we create different groups each time."

Explain that each child has a playing card. For this game, aces will count as one; jacks, queens, and kings will count as ten. All the other cards have their own numerical value (two through ten).

Say, "I'm going to name a number. When I do, connect up with other children and work together to have your cards add up to that number. For example, if I say the number fourteen, your group could have someone with a queen (ten) plus a four, or your group could have a seven plus a five plus a two. It doesn't matter how many—or how few—are in your group. What's important is that your group adds up to the right number."

Note: If you have six children or fewer present, give each child two or three cards and let them pick which card they want to use each time.

Play the game. Call out numbers between eleven and thirty. Give the children time to find groups. The last time, have all the children form one group and figure out what the total number of their group would be.

End the game by saying, "Whenever we're part of a group, we have an important role to play. Let's work together as we get to know each other more."

Colorful Names

Topic: Names
Scripture: Isaiah 43:1-7
Familiarity Between Children: None to a lot
Materials: A large piece of white butcher paper, washable markers in many colors, and blue painter's tape

Game: Clear an area and lay down a large piece of white butcher paper. (You can do this on the floor—or you can hang it up on a wall.) Give the children access to washable markers.

Say, "The book of Isaiah says that God has called each one of us by name, and each one of us belongs to God. I'd like each one of you to draw an outline of your first name on this paper. Then I want you to decorate your name in any way that you want."

Give the children time to outline and decorate their names. Encourage them to do their best work since you will display the paper on the wall.

End the activity by saying one positive thing about each child's first name. For example, you could say, "Joshua is terrific. AnnaMae is wonderful. Steffen is amazing. Jodi is caring." Then together display the name poster on a wall in your room or somewhere in your church.

Lots of Letters

Topic: Care
Scripture: Hebrews 13:1-2
Familiarity Between Children: None to a lot
Materials: A stack of 8.5 x 11-inch white paper and washable markers in many colors

A B C D E F
G H I J K L
M N O P Q
R S T U V
W X Y Z

Game: Form groups of five or six. Give each group two pieces of paper. Have the children write their first names on one piece of paper. Then have them write the alphabet from A to Z on the second piece of paper. Then have the children look at the first names on the first sheet and circle the letters on the second sheet that are included in those names. For example, if a group has two children named Nathan and Elizabeth, the children would circle a, b, e, h, i, l, n, t, and z. Then have the children total up the letters used. For Nathan and Elizabeth, it would be nine.

Form different groups. Consider putting all the boys together and all the girls together. End with making one group of all the children.

End the activity by saying, "Hebrews 13 says it's good to love and care for each other. When we work together, we invite each other into our lives."

Good Wishes

Topic: Love
Scripture: Matthew 22:37-39
Familiarity Between Children: Some to a lot
Materials: A manila envelope for each child, a stack of 8.5 x 11-inch white paper, washable markers in many colors, and blue painter's tape

Game: Give each child a manila envelope. Have each child write his or her name in large letters on the envelope. (Older children may need to help younger children.) Then hang the envelopes around the room so that they surround you in a circle.

If you have a small group (seven children or fewer), have the children create a note or picture for each child present. Do this by first having each child write the first name of each other child on a separate piece of paper and create a stack. Have the children mix up the stack of paper so that not all the children are working on something for the same child.

If you have a large group (eight children or more), have the children create a note or picture for four different children. Make sure that you have an equal number for each child so that the well-known children don't get more than the lesser-known children.

Give the children time to either write a short note or draw a picture for each child. Once the children have finished, have them stand. Say, "Going clockwise, I want you to skip and deliver your mail to the right envelope." Give the children some time to do this. Periodically have the children change direction and move in a different way, such as tiptoe, hop, walk backward, or shuffle their feet as they move sideways.

Once the children have finished, have them sit. End the activity by giving each child his or her envelope. Say, "The Bible says it is good to love each other. We show our love for each other by being kind and giving notes to each other." Let the children open up their envelopes and see what's inside.

98

Fabulous Families

Topic: Family
Scripture: Numbers 1
Familiarity Between Children: A little to a lot
Materials: A paper cup for each child filled with eight differ-
ent colored M&M® candies and a plastic spoon

Game: Give each child a paper cup filled with M&M® candies
and a plastic spoon. Say, "In the Bible, the book of Numbers
tells about all kinds of different families. Each one of us lives in
a family, and we're going to play a game to learn more about
our families."

Explain that each child will walk around the room and talk
to other people. They cannot eat any of their candy until they
have a cup of all the same-colored candies. When partners
have answered the current question, they can exchange candies with their spoons, but only after they say their names and
answer the question. Say that you will periodically change the
question.

Start with this question: Who are the people in your family?

Give the children time to do the activity. Occasionally change
the question, using questions like these:

- What do you enjoy doing best with your family?
- Who is your favorite person in your family? Why?
- What does your family do during the holidays?
- What do you wish your family had more time to do?
- Does your family have pets? If so, what are they? If not,
  why not?
- What do people in your family do to make you laugh?

Once the children have finished, let them eat their candy.
End the activity by saying, "Whether we have small or big
families, our families help us become who we are meant to be
and give us a home."

Tied Together

Topic: Neighbors
Scripture: 2 John 5
Familiarity Between Children: None to a lot
Materials: A piece of two-foot-long yarn or string for each
child and scissors

Game: Read aloud 2 John 5. Talk about how it's good to know each other and care for each other. When we're good neighbors, we're loving and caring.

Have each child find a partner, preferably someone he or she does not know well. Have one person tie one end of his or her yarn to each wrist. Have the other person loop his or her yarn through the partner's yarn before tying the ends to his or her own wrists. That way partners should be connected.

Once all the partners are connected, have partners say their first names to each other. Then instruct them to do the following (which will be tricky as they both try to do these things at the same time):

- Pat your neighbor's head
- Touch your neighbor's toes
- Massage your neighbor's shoulders
- Tickle your neighbor
- Touch your neighbor's nose
- Hug your neighbor

Once the children have finished, cut partners apart. Say, "When we're connected to each other, we work together to do the right thing. This week, let's be good neighbors to each other."

The Helping Tree

Topic: Helping
Scripture: Psalm 121
Familiarity Between Children: None to a lot
Materials: A pad of 1.5 x 2-inch sticky notes, a beanbag, a
washable marker, and a tree with lots of branches
drawn on a large piece of paper and secured to
the wall

Game: Before you play this game, draw a tree on a large piece of paper and hang it on the wall. Make sure the tree has lots of branches. Place a pad of sticky notes and a marker near the tree.

Have the children sit in a circle. Say, "Psalm 121 says our help comes from the Lord. We also can do our part to help. There's a pad of sticky notes and a marker sitting near the tree. We're going to play a game with the beanbag. We're going to toss the beanbag from person to person. When I say, 'stop,' whoever has the beanbag has to say his or her name and one way he or she has helped someone. When it's your turn, say your name and one way you have helped someone. Then get up, go to the sticky notes, write your name on one of the notes, and place it onto one of the branches of the tree. Then come back to the circle and join in the game."

Once a child has said something and jumped up, continue playing the game so that children are often getting up and sitting down at the same time. If a child gets named a second time, he or she can say a different way he or she has helped someone.

End the game by saying, "Look at all the names on our helping tree! God likes it when we help each other, and God always helps us when we need it

Looking for MORE GREAT GAMES?

101 Great Games for Kids by Jolene L. Roehlkepartain is the original games book that brought scripture to life by getting kids up and moving. Divided into four sections, *101 Great Games for Kids* includes easy-to-use games for preschoolers, children in grades K–3, children in grades 4–6, and groups of mixed-aged children. A scripture guide provides quick help in locating specific Bible passages. ISBN 978-0-687-08795-2

101 Great Games for Infants, Toddlers, and Preschoolers by Jolene L. Roehlkepartain highlights creative ways to play with young children from birth to age 5. Each game includes a scripture passage, a teaching point, a supervision tip, materials needed, and easy-to-use game instructions. Even as babies are beginning to crawl, toddlers are learning to speak, and preschoolers are starting to cooperate with play-mates, they can begin to discover God's word and God's world through play. ISBN 978-0-687-00814-8

101 More Great Games for Kids by Jolene L. Roehlkepartain presents 101 new games based on scripture to play with children from ages three through twelve. Find twenty-five games for preschoolers (ages 3–5), twenty-five games for young elementary children (grades K–3), twenty-five games for older elementary children (grades 4–6), and twenty-six games for mixed-age groups (grades K–6).
ISBN 978-0-687-33407-0

Learn more about Jolene's books through her website: www.BooksbyJolene.com

101 Great Games for Kids, 101 Great Games for Infants, Toddlers, and Preschoolers, and *101 More Great Games for Kids* are all available from Abingdon Press, Nashville, Tennessee.

Scripture Index

TOPICAL INDEX